RACE, PREJUDICE AND EDUCATION

by

Cyril Bibby

HEINEMANN

LONDON

Heinemann Educational Books Ltd
LONDON MELBOURNE TORONTO
SINGAPORE CAPE TOWN
AUCKLAND IBADAN
HONG KONG

FIRST PUBLISHED IN THE UNITED KINGDOM 1959
REPRINTED 1960, 1964

PUBLISHED BY
HEINEMANN EDUCATIONAL BOOKS LTD
15-16 QUEEN STREET, MAYFAIR, LONDON W.1
PRINTED IN GREAT BRITAIN FOR THE PUBLISHERS BY
BUTLER AND TANNER LTD, FROME AND LONDON

'No branches of historical inquiry have suffered more from fanciful speculation than those which relate to the origin and attributes of the races of mankind.'

Lord Bryce

'Of all the vulgar modes of escaping from the consideration of the effects of social and moral influences on the human mind, the most vulgar is that of attributing the diversities of conduct and character to inherent natural differences.'

John Stuart Mill

'Homo sum: humani nihil a me alienum puto.'

Terence

ABOUT THIS BOOK

This book is an outcome of the Seventh Session of the General Conference of Unesco, which authorised the Director-General to continue to assemble and disseminate knowledge likely to combat racial prejudice.

Since most prejudices are acquired during childhood, in the home or on the playground, a campaign against racialism could not be aimed exclusively at adults. For this reason Unesco decided to initiate the preparation of books specially designed to help school teachers. These books would provide the scientific information on which simple teaching about race must be based, together with some guidance on how to use this information to overcome racial prejudice in the minds of their pupils.

Dr. Cyril Bibby was therefore invited in 1953 to prepare a manuscript on these lines, and the first draft was submitted for comment to an international committee of social scientists and educators. The text was revised by the author in the light of these comments, and finally emerged in the form in which it is here published.

Since countries differ in their experience of the problem of race relations, which in some places is acute and in others almost unknown, no one text can suit all regions of the world. Dr. Bibby's book is specially adapted to conditions in the United Kingdom, but has also been circulated by Unesco to all its Member States so that they may consider whether similar books, perhaps based on it, could be prepared for use in their countries.

CONTENTS

Page 1 2 3 4 5 [illegible]

A O T A

Chapter 10 and
Chapter 11

Chapter 2

Chapt. 13

Introduction

Any booklet of this size must take certain things for granted if it is to deal at all adequately with other things, and perhaps it would be as well to say at the outset what is taken for granted here. We assume, then, that the teacher who reads these pages needs no convincing of the fundamental wrongness of those beliefs and actions which led in the past to the enslavement of Negroes and in our own time to the genocide of Jews. We assume also that, leaving aside questions of political or social expediency, he would disapprove in principle of discrimination merely on grounds of ethnic origin. And, finally, we assume that, if he can become conscientiously convinced that there is no rational ground for any kind of racial prejudice, he will wish to do all he can to free himself and his pupils from it.

The teacher who wishes to deal honestly with race and race relations may sometimes find himself in a difficult situation. The domestic policy of his own state in relation to racial discrimination, or its foreign policy in relation to colonial administration, may appear to the teacher eminently worthy of criticism. What is he to do in these circumstances? It is not merely that he might find himself in trouble if he expressed his views too frankly: there is the much more important fact that it is a recognized responsibility of members of the teaching profession to refrain from pressing their own opinions too strongly on their pupils. This is a problem to which there is no simple or generalized solution; and no one can relieve the individual teacher, who knows the individual school and the individual pupils, of the responsibility of making his own decisions in the light of local circumstances. But one thing may be said in general: the teacher must be sure that he does not allow social cowardice to masquerade as professional integrity or sell his soul for prospects of promotion.

Teachers are the target of enthusiasts for every cause and, if they were to try to include in the school curriculum everything which the various enthusiasts have suggested, there would be no end to their teaching. It is quite impossible to find time in school to teach children everything that one would wish, and it is not the intention of this handbook to suggest that teachers should incorporate in their lessons everything that it might be useful for children to know about race. But there are some facts which are so important, and which fit so naturally into a normal lesson framework, that schools should ensure that their pupils are made aware of them.

Yet education is a much more complex thing than mere factual instruction: it is concerned not only with imparting knowledge but also with influencing behaviour, and human behaviour is motivated at least as much by sentiment as by reason. Thus, apart from the comparatively straightforward job of telling children the elementary facts of race, teachers are faced with the much more subtle task of eroding undesirable racial prejudices and establishing sentiments of human kinship that will transcend all ethnic boundaries. This task is not to be accomplished in a few set lessons, but will require a long and patient process of sympathetic guidance. And most powerful of all will be the implicit assumptions and overt actions of the teacher himself, who by one exhibition of colour prejudice will set at nought any number of lessons on the biology of human variation and by a single anti-Semitic sneer will negate innumerable affirmations of human equality.

This matter of education in race relations is of concern not only to those teachers who live and work in areas where racial discrimination is rife; there are very few places, even in lands with a proud history of toleration, where beneath the smooth surface there is not some undercurrent of racial prejudice. The Negro has the same rights of admission to hotels in Britain as any other person, but he may frequently find that all their rooms are 'already occupied'. The Algerian may be a citizen of France, but his path will be harder than that of a fellow-citizen of lighter hue. The Jew may distinguish himself in an American university, but certain student fraternities will be closed to him. And, contrariwise, the Gentile may be held in low esteem by the Jew, and the European despised by the very African or Asian on whom he himself looks down.

One of the difficulties in any discussion of race relations is that of definition. From a purely academic point of view, it might be better to wait until biologists and anthropologists and sociologists have produced a unanimous definition of 'race', but the matter is not simply an academic one. Racial prejudice and discrimination are present and urgent evils, and racial tension and friction have mounted menacingly in our own generation. Moreover, a firm belief in something which is not a fact is itself a fact, and there can be 'racial prejudice' against a group which is not a 'race'. We cannot, therefore, delay action indefinitely while awaiting definition.

Perhaps an extreme case of this difficulty relates to the Jewish people. They certainly do not constitute a race in any proper sense, and it might be argued that anti-Semitism should not be considered in the same context as colour prejudice; but, despite the objective differences between them, these two phenomena have many subjective features in common. Nevertheless, it should be stated explicitly that the joint treatment here of anti-Semitism and colour prejudice must not be taken to imply that the distinction between Jew and Gentile is of the same nature as that between Negroid and Caucasoid and Mongoloid.

Yet, from another point of view, the field covered in this booklet might be criticized as being too narrow rather than too wide. There are resemblances between racial tension and other intergroup tensions, such as those between different religious groups and different social classes, or those between rural and urban populations, or those between well-established inhabitants and newcomers to the community. And, there seems little doubt, these different types of tension may be increased by similar forces and might be diminished by parallel procedures. Had space been unlimited, this handbook could have been much improved by the addition of a full treatment of the problems of intergroup relations in general, but it would thereby have become a very large volume. It is hoped that readers will bear in mind this limitation and continually remind themselves that racial prejudice will not be dissolved if it is treated entirely in isolation.

Conditions vary so enormously from country to country,

and even in different communities within the one country, that it is impossible to lay down any universally applicable rules about how to combat racial prejudice and encompass racial understanding. Techniques which have been developed in one civilization may not easily be introduced into the schools of another; and it will be necessary in each culture to study the state of existing race attitudes and feelings, to estimate the role which the schools can reasonably be expected to play, to test the readiness of teachers to take part in this process of education and re-education, to prepare educational material adapted to local needs, and to work out in detail the ways in which the job can best be done. But it is hoped that, provided it is read in the spirit in which it is written, as making only general suggestions requiring adaptation to particular circumstances, this booklet may be of some value to teachers who wish to play their part in this great humanizing task.

All too often, however, when society is faced with a problem of human behaviour or social relations, there is a tendency to assume that its solution can be left to the schools. Teachers, generally speaking, are conscientious people with a sharp sense of social obligation, and they are usually prepared to play their part in any urgent social task. But their part in eradicating racial prejudice, although important, is only a part; and the school can be wholly successful only if society at large plays its part also. While, therefore, this handbook may be helpful to teachers in planning their lessons and reconsidering the regimen of their schools, its purpose will only be fully realized if, in addition, it leads to the organization of much wider action. In each country, perhaps, a committee might be constituted (that is, where no appropriate organization already exists) with the specific aim of co-ordinating a wide range of activities directed to the diminution of racial tension. A series of articles in educational journals could secure the interest of a much larger number of teachers than is likely to have read this booklet (and may prompt many of them to do so), and other articles in national and local newspapers could make millions of mothers and fathers familiar with what the teachers of their children are trying to do. Teachers' trade unions and professional organizations might make this matter the subject of discussion at conferences and branch meetings, women's guilds and co-operative societies and local adult groups of all kinds might be offered the services of speakers and discussion leaders. National and local education authorities might organize vacation schools and study courses; university departments and colleges of education could ensure that the matter is considered by those who are training tomorrow's teachers. Writers and publishers of educational textbooks could be brought together to work out ways in which their products might be improved, suitable films and filmstrips and visual material of all kinds could be prepared, radio and television producers could be made aware of the immense contribution which they could make. And, in communities where there is any sort of racial discrimination, liberally minded citizens could come together to work for its dissolution.

All this will demand not only time but also money. Perhaps it is not too much to hope that there will be public bodies and private benefactors who will count such money well spent.

1. The Use of the Word 'Race'

The fact of human ethnic variation is an elementary one, obvious to any child so soon as he first observes a person of notably different skin colour or hair type or nose shape. The pale unevenly coloured skin and rather sharp face, the narrow nose and thin lips of the European, are so markedly different from the features of his own parents that the African child cannot fail to note them; and vice versa. But what the child does not know, and what even many educated adults do not seem to know, is that it is quite impossible to mark off nkind into a few simple and clearly delineated groups on basis of such physical differences.

The concept of 'race', originating in this recognition of obvious physical distinctions between different human groups, has been developed by anthropologists as a device for classifying populations. And, as often happens when a concept is extended beyond its original range, this development of the idea of race has produced many difficulties. Some anthropologists distinguish few 'races', others distinguish many; and it is hard to find two anthropologists who completely agree in their classifications. Moreover, the popular idea of racial classification is so out of touch with the biological facts of human variation that some people would prefer to abandon entirely the use of the word 'race' in connexion with the human species.

Unfortunately, the word seems too well established for abandonment; and alternatives such as 'ethnic group' or 'genetically distinguishable populations' are too cumbersome for general acceptance into common speech. Thus, the teacher had better turn his efforts to showing his pupils how to use the word 'race' more exactly and to freeing their minds of the prejudices which the word so often carries with it.

The teacher of biology, dealing in the ordinary course of his lessons with species and their varieties, might well consider the main divisions of mankind. The native African and the native European, the native of China and the aboriginal native of Australia, differ sufficiently to warrant their being placed in distinguishable subgroups of the human species; and, providing that one does not imagine that the boundaries between them are hard and fast, these great subgroups may be not too inaccurately called 'races'. Children are not ostriches, and honest recognition of biological variation is not intolerance.

But, having dealt with this convenient use of the word 'race', the biology teacher should go on to deal with undesirable and inexact uses of the word. Every experienced teacher knows that, when explaining to children what a word means, it is often necessary also to explain what it does not mean, and the word 'race' is no exception. On these grounds

—strictly educational grounds—the teacher should explain that there is no biological warrant at all for such terms as 'the Aryan race', 'the British race', 'the Jewish race', 'the Arab race' and so on. 'Aryan' is a linguistic term for a hypothetical early language, 'British' is a political term for a particular group of nations sharing certain historical traditions and constitutional forms, 'Jewish' is a socio-theological term for people with an ancient religious tradition and with recognizable customs, 'Arab' is an ecological term for those who lead or have comparatively recently led a particular type of semi-nomadic life in the Middle East. None of these are 'races' in any proper biological sense: indeed, to speak of an 'Aryan race' is as great an abuse of words as to speak of a 'black-skinned language', and this should be made clear to children.

Similarly, the 'Jewish race' is a myth. There are people called Jews, and these people are sometimes recognizable as such, but that does not make them into a race. An Englishman travelling in the U.S.A. finds that he is commonly recognized as English, and the American in Europe is also usually recognized as such, but that does not mean that there is an 'English race' or an 'American race'. Style of dress, type of gesture, habits of hygiene, turns of speech—all these things, dependent on social environment rather than on biological heredity, combine to facilitate recognition of the members of a cultural group. And that is, primarily, what Jews are: a cultural group sharing a common religious tradition, a common sacred language, and a great wealth of common customs. There are characteristically Jewish gestures, a characteristically Jewish pattern of family life, certain characteristically Jewish occupations and cultural interests, but there is no Jewish race.

It is true that through the centuries there has been a good deal of in-breeding among the Jews in various regions, with a consequent tendency to the development of some local biological similarities. However, the combination of physical features (such as dark hair and eyes, and prominent aquiline nose) which is often described as 'Jewish' is, in fact, quite common among the peoples of Asia Minor and Eastern

Europe; and the only reason why Western Europeans often think of such features as being 'Jewish' is that unless they travel they rarely see non-Jews with these facial features. But by no means all Jews are of this physical type. Despite all barriers, they have intermarried a good deal with other peoples, and the Jews are ethnically very mixed. Many are fair-haired and some are red-haired, some are long-headed and some are short-headed, many have blue or light grey eyes, many have straight or squat noses, a few are entirely Negroid and others entirely Mongoloid in physical characteristics. The teacher, therefore, is on safe ground in correcting any of his pupils who speak of a 'Jewish race'. One may properly speak of 'the Jewish religion' or of 'the Jewish people', but never of 'the Jewish race'.

Nor is this a purely pedantic point. It is partly because the word 'race' has been so loosely used in the past, sometimes to denote biological groups and sometimes linguistic groups or religious groups, and because inexact use of language encourages inexact ideas of all kinds, that mankind has been led into racial prejudice and discrimination. Intolerance and cruelty and exploitation are things too ugly to be willingly accepted by most decent people: they have to be wrapped up in an ideological dressing which will disguise their ugliness, and muddled ideas of race have often provided such a dressing. At various times the French, the English and the Germans have all been claimed as 'Aryans', and in Nazi Germany the myths of an 'Aryan race' and a 'Jewish race' were twin strands in an elaborate pattern of prejudice, discrimination, cruelty and finally mass-murder. Therefore, the teacher who persuades his pupils—if they use it at all in a human context—to use the word 'race' exactly, is helping them also to see the world about them more clearly. Moreover, an understanding of how loosely and inaccurately the word 'race' is often employed may well be the first step to the exertion of some rational control over the emotional feelings which the word so often arouses.

2. The Complexity of Race

Teachers will often find that their pupils have fixed and over-simplified ideas (*stereotypes,* as they are called) about race. They may imagine, for example, that all Negroes and only Negroes have 'woolly' hair, or that all Chinese and only Chinese have 'slanting' eyes, or that all Scandinavians are tall and blond and blue-eyed. We need not be surprised that children in ethnically uniform areas hold such ideas, for their personal contacts provide no evident corrective to the verbal and visual over-simplifications which impinge on them from all the media of mass communication. It is, however, a little more surprising that children living in cosmopolitan cities, which count people of all colours and ethnic origins among their citizens, may also have similar false stereotypes. Evidently, social barriers may be almost as effective obstacles to understanding as those of geography, and the distance from Park Avenue to Harlem may in this sense be as great as that from Berlin to Addis Ababa. Even where children of different colours and different ethnic origins sit in the same classroom, the scales of prejudice may still so obstruct the pupils' vision as to prevent them from recognizing what is plain there for them to see.

It is similarly easy to make false generalizations about 'racial character' on the basis of observed or imagined behaviour, and we may find many of our pupils with false ideas of this kind. Thus, the European child may believe that Negroes are lazy and violent in nature, the Gentile child may imagine that Jews have natures mercantile and mean, while the Jewish child may take Gentiles to be crude and unimaginative. The child of the colonial settler may assume that the natives are naturally unintelligent and servile, while the child of the native may imagine that the settlers are naturally harsh and overbearing. In Germany there may be a favourable stereotype of 'the clean and clever Nordic' and an unfavourable sterotype of 'the unctuous and unreliable Mediterranean'; in England one may hear of 'the sensible and level-headed Anglo-Saxon' and 'the temperamental and unreliable Celt'; and today, in many parts of the Western world, there seems to be emerging an equally unjustified stereotype of 'the crafty and cruel Slav'. Without denying that peoples vary in many ways—and, indeed, while emphasizing that such variation may be a source of great cultural richness—the teacher can do much to make his pupils aware of the unreality of most stereotypes. 'Racial character' is a concept which courts confusion: the sooner children can be freed from it, the better.

The idea of 'race' is a very complex one, with elements belonging to biology, psychology, sociology, anthropology, geography and history; and it is quite impossible to give any short account of it without running the risk of dangerous over-simplification. However, it is possible to clear away fairly quickly some of the lumber of myth and fallacy which obscures the essential facts.[1] The major fallacy which bedevils any proper understanding of the situation is the simple—but false—idea that mankind can be split into a number of quite distinct divisions characterized by clear-cut biological differences. Naturally, if a school uses atlases which include population maps based on the Blumenbach or similar system of 'black, brown, yellow, red and white races', the teacher will need to point out their utter fallaciousness.

In fact, the biological classification of our species is a matter of great complexity. If skin colour is taken as a criterion, the natives of Africa and Australia fall in one group and those of Europe in another; but, if hairiness of body be the criterion, the European falls with the aboriginal Australians, while the African must be placed in a group apart. Use cephalic index as a guide, and one finds long-heads and short-heads mixed up together the whole world over; use blood-group distribution, and yet other affiliations are indicated. A classification of mankind by one biological criterion

1. Some of the commoner misconceptions about race are discussed in an interesting way by Juan Comas in his booklet *Racial Myths,* published by Unesco (Paris, 1951).

does not correspond with the classification which results from using another criterion; and it is impossible to say, of any one particular criterion, 'This is the right one.' Recognizing this, anthropologists take account of all these characteristics in combination; and, even then, it is still very difficult to decide to what ethnic group some individuals belong.

3. The Main Divisions of Mankind

Although scientists have been unable to agree among themselves upon any one scheme for the ethnic classification of mankind, teachers can nevertheless present to their pupils a picture that is fairly simple and not too inaccurate. This picture will have three main components, repeatedly intermingling but none the less distinguishable. These three main components are the Mongoloid peoples, the Caucasoid peoples and the Negroid peoples. There are, in addition, other groups (such as the Bushmen of South Africa, the Ainus of Japan, the Negritoes of the Congo and the Pacific, and the aboriginal inhabitants of Australia) who do not easily fit into this threefold classification; but, for the sake of simplicity, no more is said about them here.

The Mongoloids are the peoples often referred to as 'Asians' or 'the yellow races', but both these terms are misleading. The members of this group spread far beyond Asia, over Oceania and the two Americas; while on the other hand, many Asians (for example, most Indians) do not belong to the group at all. Nor do most members of the group have skin which could properly be called 'yellow': its colour may range from a hue paler than that of many Italians to a deep bronze reddish-brown. The Mongoloid peoples tend to have broad and rather flat faces, with high cheekbones and a fold of flesh at the inner corner of the eye which makes it look somewhat slit-like and slanting; but by no means all members of the group have all these characteristics. Their noses are usually of medium breadth and not often high-bridged, and their eyes tend to be brown or blackish-brown in colour. They commonly have only sparse body hair; while the hair of their heads is usually dark brown or black in colour, thick in texture and straight in conformation. But to every one of these general tendencies there are exceptions.

The Caucasoids are the peoples often referred to as 'Europeans' or 'the white races', but these terms are even more misleading than the corresponding terms for the Mongoloids. In the first place (and quite apart from the descendants of European colonizers, who have spread over the face of the earth during the last five centuries) the Caucasoid peoples cover not only most of Europe but also great areas of North Africa, the Near East and India. In the second place, these peoples are not white: their skin colour ranges from pale pink to a deep ruddy hue, from a pale olive colour to a definite brown. This point is worth emphasizing, because when a child realizes that a dark-skinned Indian belongs to the same main ethnic group as a pale European, and not to the same group as a dark African, he may begin to see that the colour-bar is as illogical as it is immoral. The Caucasoids are perhaps the most variable of the three great ethnic groups. Just as their skin colour may range from pale pink to dark brown, their eyes may range from pale blue to deep sepia, and their hair from almost white to black. However, their profiles are usually fairly straight, with a mouth that does not project; while their lips are normally thin and their noses relatively narrow and high-bridged. They have commonly a good deal of body hair, and the hair of their heads is in texture fine to medium and in conformation straight to wavy.

The Negroids are the peoples often referred to as 'Africans' or 'the black races', but here again the common geographical and chromatic terms are misleading. Members of this great group occur not only in Africa, but also (and quite apart from relatively recent population movements to America and elsewhere) in wide areas of Oceania and even in parts of mainland Asia. Then, as to skin colour, they may range from virtually black to a quite pale yellow-brown; while their eyes and hair are commonly brown or black. Members of this group often have a rather projecting mouth and a broad and low-bridged nose, but not in all cases. Generally Negroids have very little body hair, while their head hair is usually curly and rather thick in texture.

The child who has learned these facts (and noticed how large a part such words as 'usually', 'commonly', 'normally', 'rather', 'fairly', 'tend', 'range', and 'often' play in these anthropological descriptions) can scarcely fail to realize that 'race' is not the simple, hard-and-fast matter which it is commonly taken to be. It should be noted, moreover, that these accounts of the three main ethnic groups of mankind are only descriptions, and only partial descriptions at that. They tell us nothing whatever about the ways in which the physical differences between the groups have come about, nothing about the extent to which these differences are hereditary or acquired, nothing about the basic physiological processes of the body which are so much more important than mere hair or skin colour, nothing about mental and moral and spiritual qualities. All these are matters for further study.

4. Biology and Human Variation

It is impossible even to begin to understand the nature of ethnic groups without knowing something of the ways in which individuals differ from each other, and variation between human individuals rests on the same biological bases as variation between individuals of other species. The causes of variation are many and complex, but it is quite possible to give children a clear, even if elementary, idea of them.

Probably most secondary school biology courses deal at

some point with the interrelationship between heredity and environment (or, as it is sometimes expressed, the interaction between nature and nurture), neither of which can be properly considered in isolation. Whether one considers the yield of a field of barley or the height of a boy or girl, both hereditary endowment and conditions of growth must be taken into account: it is almost meaningless to speak of a certain character as being 'produced by heredity' or 'produced by environment'. Every character is influenced in its development by both heredity and environment—in some cases mainly by the former and in other cases mainly by the latter, but often to a considerable extent by both.

The hereditary component in variation is now known to depend upon what are called *genes,* which each individual plant or animal inherits from its parents. Each gene may influence one or more processes in the living cells of the individual, and it is as a result of these processes that the individual grows as it does. A plant does not inherit red flowers as such; it inherits genes which so influence the processes going on in the cells of the plant as eventually to produce red flowers. A person does not inherit brown eyes; he inherits genes which cause his eyes to become brown. This distinction is an important one; for, so long as we think in terms of 'the inheritance of characters', it is impossible to understand the facts of biological variation. To repeat, then: it is not characters which are inherited, but genes. These genes influence the various processes in the living cells, and these processes produce the individual's characteristics.

The genes are contained in microscopic thread-like bodies called *chromosomes*; and, in the case of humans, each egg cell and each sperm cell contains 24 chromosomes. Thus, the fertilized egg from which the baby grows contains 48 chromosomes, 24 from each parent. In general, each gene from the father is matched by one from the mother, and the two genes together influence the development of this character or that. Every individual (except in the unusual case of identical twins) has a different complement of genes from every other individual, and so each one of us develops as a distinctive being with unique potentialities.

In any given population, there is a certain range of genes and, generation by generation, the total supply is 'reshuffled' into fresh groupings in the newly conceived individuals. This reservoir of genes does not remain constant, but may change in at least three ways.

First, there is *natural selection*. If a particular gene produces a character which is advantageous to the individual, facilitating his survival and production of offspring to a greater extent than his fellows, natural selection of the gene will occur and its frequency in the population as a whole will gradually increase as time goes on. And, since a gene may influence more than one character, it is possible for a character to be selected, not because it is itself advantageous, but because it happens to be associated with another character which is of advantage. Conversely, if a gene is disadvantageous, it will suffer 'negative natural selection' and gradually disappear from the population.

Second, there is what is known as *mutation*. Although as a general rule each gene reproduces itself exactly in the formation of the parents' sex cells, it sometimes happens that there is an irregularity, and the newly formed gene is different from that which has produced it. The new gene, produced by this mutation, then passes into the general reservoir and, under favourable circumstances, may multiply from generation to generation and gradually spread right through the population.

Third, there is chance fluctuation, sometimes called *genetic drift*. The sorting out of the genes in each new generation is a matter of 'chance'—which is merely a short-hand way of saying that we do not know what forces determine the sorting, but that it takes place in accordance with the expectations of the mathematics of probability. Thus, especially if the population is a small one, the chance happenings of life and death and mating and breeding may lead to some change or 'drift' in the proportion of different genes constituting the population's total reservoir.

Naturally, if two hitherto separate populations, each with its own reservoir of genes, meet and interbreed, there are yet other changes. The two gene reservoirs are now pooled, and generation by generation become more inextricably mixed.

But, however long the mixing process goes on, the individual genes retain their individuality. Each person, after the interbreeding has gone on for many generations, will have some genes which came originally from one of the two populations and some which came from the other, and will therefore be intermediate between the two populations in type. But the individual genes are still distinct: there is nothing corresponding to the popular idea of 'mixing of blood', as of two liquids diluting each other. The genes do not blend: they are merely combined in patterns like the coloured stones in a mosaic, capable of constituting many different designs but never losing their individual integrity.

This modern view of genetic processes, although complex in detail, is simple in essence and quite within the range of understanding of secondary school pupils. Biology teachers are increasingly recognizing that, while Mendel's classic experiments in the heredity of the domestic pea represent a major landmark in the history of science, it is undesirable to allow them to loom too large in school lessons. Pupils are much more interested in people than in peas, and school lessons might well deal with the elements of human heredity and variation.[1] In this way—learning how varied are the genetic patterns of a superficially homogeneous population, discovering the mechanisms which produce pigmentary differences, finding how much a child in Berlin may have in common with one in Bangkok—pupils may come to see how oversimplified are the common conceptions of 'race' and how essential it is to consider each human being as an individual rather than merely as one of a group.

---

1. An excellent reference book for the teacher is *The New You and Heredity,* by Amram Scheinfeld (Lippincott, Philadelphia, and Chatto & Windus, London, 1950).

5. The Origins of Ethnic Groups

From time to time in human history there have been suggestions about the origins of ethnic groups—theories ranging from the sublime to the ridiculous. We are still unable to speak with any certainty in the matter; but it is possible, by combining our knowledge of observed group differences with our knowledge of the biological basis of variation, to draw some conclusions which have a fair degree of probability. And when, as is almost certain to happen at some time, children raise the matter in the classroom, it would be well for them to be given the essentials of such conclusions.

Although most secondary school biology courses make mention of the theory of evolution, some teachers, fearing to offend religious susceptibilities, refrain from referring to the evolution of our own species. Today, however, most religious leaders agree that the biological facts of evolution in no way conflict with the essentials of religion, and in any case this issue should not be evaded. Other teachers, while dealing with the evolution of *Homo sapiens* as a species, omit consideration of the evolution of our different ethnic groupings —although this is a fascinating topic, which might well form part of a school course in biology.

Our species probably evolved from some ape-like forebear, perhaps in Asia or perhaps in Africa, and was at the time of its first appearance only one of several different species of man-like creatures. However, perhaps because they could not compete with the superior intelligence of *Homo sapiens,* the other man-like species eventually disappeared, and we remained as 'lords of creation'. In those early days, dependent on wild plants and animals for their food, relying upon caves for shelter and skins for clothes, unprotected from the elements and living lives of constant danger, the human population of the earth must have been very small indeed.

If this population had remained ever in contact, without any barriers to breeding among its members, there would never have arisen the various ethnic groups which are often called 'races'. Naturally, individuals would have differed from each other in all sorts of ways, but these differences would have been distributed more or less at random throughout the population. Distinct ethnic groups could only come into existence as a result of the separation of mankind into isolated populations, between which there was little or no interbreeding over fairly long periods of time. This separation may have been brought about in various ways, but probably the chief cause was the formation of great barriers of frozen wasteland during a glacial period long ago. And, once separated into isolated groups, our species began the process of differentiation into recognizably different groups. Children may naturally ask 'where did the different "races" originate?' and the teacher must answer as well as he can.

Some scientists believe that Asia, the great central land mass of the world, is the home of the different human groups. According to this theory, the Caucasoids developed during a period of isolation somewhere in the region of Persia and Afghanistan, the Mongoloids further to the east but north of the Himalaya, the Negroids and Australoids south of the Himalaya in India or thereabouts. Many years later, when the great ice-barrier had melted away, some Caucasoids probably went north and west to populate Europe and North Africa, while others went south and east to people India. The Mongoloids went east and north and south, populating most of Asia, and then over the Behring Straits to America. Similarly, according to this theory, the Australoids and Negroids, perhaps under pressure from invading Caucasoids, left India and set out across the sea; the former south to Australia, and the latter west to Africa and east to Melanesia. There are, however, other theories of the origin of the great ethnic divisions of mankind—one being that the Negroids originated in Africa—and the teacher should make it clear to his pupils that no one really knows for certain the answer to their question.

Most children would share the popular belief that the so-called 'racial' differences are adaptive in character, and no doubt this is partly true. Thus, for example, dark pigmentation, which protects the skin from the fierce rays of the sun, is seen predominantly in the peoples of Africa and the tropical east; and it may well be that skin colour originally evolved as an adaptation to climate. On the other hand, the Amerindians, with much the same degree of skin pigmentation from Baffin Island to Tierra del Fuego, can live healthily alike in wintry waste and gentle grassland and steaming forest; so there is no necessary connexion between colour and climate. Similarly, it may be that the broader nostrils of the Negroids, allowing easy access of air to the lungs, are more suited to people living in a land of warm air; while the narrower nostrils of the Caucasoids, slowing down the access of air to the lungs, are more suited to people living in a land of cold air. But we are not certain that this is so. And, in any event, it could scarcely be suggested that some regional characteristics, such as the Mongoloid eye-fold, have any particular adaptive significance.

The honest thing for the teacher to say, therefore, is that we know very little for certain about why different peoples have skins of this colour or that, or noses narrow or flat, or hair straight or curly. In some cases we can feel fairly certain that a character represents an adaptation to climate, in other cases equally confident that it is not so, in most cases very hesitant about what our answer should be. But the two essential facts are clear, and quite capable of being understood by schoolchildren: when populations are isolated from each other, differences tend to develop between them; when populations mix, the differences between them tend to diminish. And, so far back as our knowledge goes, such isolation and such admixture have been going on among humans intermittently and in varying degrees, so that we may speak not of the 'origin' of ethnic groups, but only of their 'origins'.

6. The Nature of Group Differences

Teachers will probably find that many of their pupils think of the so-called human 'races' as being similar to the races or subspecies which exist in many common plants and animals, and this misapprehension must be removed. The definite varieties of naturally occurring species are believed to have developed largely as a result of natural selection during long-continued isolation, while those of domesticated species have been artificially selected by plant and animal breeders; and, in either case, comparatively little interbreeding has taken place to erode the sharp edges of the distinct varieties. But the position in the case of humans is quite different: so far as our knowledge goes, there has never been a time when some mingling of adjacent groups has not taken place; and the varieties of mankind are not static, but dynamic, ever changing and ever mixing. As a result, there is nothing in humans to correspond with the sharply defined differences between the varieties of many other species, and this should be made very clear to children.

Similarly, whenever a suitable opportunity occurs, whether the school lesson be biology or geography or social studies or any other subject, children should learn something of the wide range of individual differences within each of the main ethnic groupings. The European child who knows that the Indian belongs to the same major group as himself, that Negroes vary among themselves as much as 'Whites' do, and that the Chinese may at first find it as difficult to distinguish individual Europeans as Europeans do to distinguish individual Chinese, may begin to appreciate the deceptive nature of racial stereotypes.

But, even when a child realizes that the members of an ethnic group differ widely from each other, he may still have a false conception of the nature of human variation. He may tend to regard the narrow-nosed Negro as being not a 'pure' Negroid, or the dark-skinned Indian as being not a 'pure' Caucasoid; and he must learn that this notion of an 'ideal racial type' does not correspond to reality. If one speaks to a child about a horse, he summons up a mental image which is, as it were, a composite photograph of all the horses he ever saw; but he will readily recognize that the shaggy-coated heavy-footed plough horse, and the smooth-skinned high-stepping hunter, are no less genuinely horses than the 'average horse' which he has visualized. In the same way, those members of any human ethnic group who differ from the average are no less genuinely members of the group than those who happen to present the average picture. The so-called 'pure member of a race', the 'ideal racial type', is nothing more than a composite visual image of the average, and it is important that children should realize this. It might be a useful exercise to present to the class a 'typical picture' of a school-child, and then compare this stereotype with each member of the class in turn. In this way, the children might come to see that scarcely one of them corresponds closely to the 'type', yet each would maintain that he is none the less a genuine schoolchild. Similarly, American children might compare the adults of their acquaintance with 'Uncle Sam' and British children with 'John Bull'. By a series of exercises of this sort, designed to display the inadequacy of stereotypes of familiar groups close at hand, pupils might perceive the danger of stereotypes in general and so come to look more realistically at the members of other ethnic groups. And, most valuably, they might more fully appreciate the importance of considering each individual as an individual, rather than merely as a specimen of a group.

In addition to such qualitative indications of the wide variation within each ethnic group, it may be possible to give pupils some understanding of the quantitative aspects of such variation. Since so much in the modern world is counted and measured and computed, and since so many social and political problems are presented to the public in statistical terms, it is important for our children to learn the language of variation. Teachers of mathematics, therefore, are subjecting their traditional curricula to critical examination, and seeking ways of introducing simple statistics into schools. A start may be made by showing that, in some circumstances, an average without a range of variation may be not merely useless but positively misleading. The ingenious teacher will find all sorts of ways to illustrate this point. One simple approach is by the study of the weather, which soon makes clear how little value is an average temperature without a temperature range. Or the class may plot distribution curves from the heights and weights of the children in the class, or from the scores made by darts aimed at a miniature archery target, or from a hundred and one other examples of random distribution.

A great deal of useful numerical material[1] is also available in connexion with ethnic resemblances and differences; and, in particular, when the teacher of mathematics is explaining to his pupils the nature of the 'normal curve', he can find admirable material in human ethnology. A school class which has studied the statistics of human variation can no longer imagine that an individual is adequately described merely by the average characteristics of his group.

A good example of the way in which populations may differ in the relative commonness of certain biological traits is found in the facts of blood grouping.[2] To the warm and generous mind of adolescence, the giving of one's blood to save the life of a fellow-human is an act which makes an immediate imaginative appeal, and the fact that in blood transfusion the skin colours of the giver and the receiver are entirely irrelevant may be a potent solvent of racial prejudice. Pale-faced John's blood may be unsuitable to give to his own sister Jane, but may be suited to black-skinned Nkruma and to yellow-skinned Chiang; and such facts illustrate dramatically that our human individuality is more important than our ethnic affiliation. True, the proportions of children having blood of the different groups may vary from one population to another; but the essential point is that *some* children from the one population may have blood of the same type as *some* children from the other, and of different type from other

---

1. Some of which is given in G. M. Morant's booklet *The Significance of Racial Differences,* published by Unesco (Paris, 1952).
2. A simple account is given in L. C. Dunn's booklet *Race and Biology,* published by Unesco (Paris, 1951).

children in their own population. In the basic matter of blood there are no sharp national or ethnic boundaries.

Evidently, since a 'pink' man could be pumped full of the blood of a 'black' or 'yellow' man of the proper blood group and vice versa with no harmful effect, any physiological differences which may exist between the human ethnic groups are of less importance than the differences between individuals within a group. Similarly, in all populations there are bright and dull, good and evil, miserly and generous, jovial and morose, mad and sane, kind and cruel. Mr. A. from Accra may be black, Mr. B. from Birmingham pink, Mr. C. from Canton yellow and Mr. D. from Delhi brown; but, in the context of the overwhelming similarity between all humans, these facts about skin colour are comparatively trivial. Similarly, in this context, variations in texture of hair, or shape of nose, or fullness of lips signify little. In garden flowers, which are bred for visual effect, pigmentation may be the chief point; in sheep, bred for their wool, hair texture is important. But in humans, where the one great important fact is their common humanity, such differences fade into insignificance. This is not to deny the existence of differences, nor even to discourage honest recognition of it: it is only to do what we must ever do, to evaluate the facts once they have been recognized.

Even such a comparatively simple characteristic as skin colour may be influenced by environment as well as by hereditary factors; but, when we come to consider the immensely more complex matter of temperament and personality, the importance of environment becomes almost overwhelming. There are, of course, genetic differences. No one who keeps his eyes open can be in the slightest doubt that one person may inherit a tendency to a somewhat placid temperament and another a tendency to excitability, but it is equally clear that many differences in human personality are determined more by nurture than by nature. And, certainly, even the most cursory study of comparative anthropology makes it impossible to ascribe the immense observed variation of accepted behaviour to innate biological traits or so-called 'racial character'.

Some indication of the powerful way in which society may mould the individual temperament, and cause this or that pattern of behaviour to become common, is given by the strikingly different cultures of the North American Indians.[1] The tribes concerned all belong to the same major division of the Mongoloid peoples, and what small biological differences there may be between them show no particular correlation with their remarkably diversified values and institutions. There is, despite their general similarity of biological inheritance, remarkably little in attitudes and behaviour common to, for example, the Pueblo Indians of the south-western desert and the Kwakiutl Indians of the north-western coast.

Less than a century ago, up on the north-west coast, the Kwakiutl Indians led a life of dramatic competitiveness. Individual status was all-important, one man's dignity was increased by the shaming of another, and loss of status could be compensated only in some extravagant gesture such as the distribution or destruction of property or even suicide. Possessions were industriously accumulated, not for utility but as a means of shaming the less wealthy, and at the great ceremonial feasts chiefs would vie in acts and speeches of self-glorification. Dancing was dionysian, with mouth-frothing and the doing of terrible deeds in frenzy. Supernatural prerogatives were obtained by hallucinatory visions, induced by drugs or fasting or self-inflicted agony—or they might be gained more simply by murdering one who had them. The gods were envisaged as hostile, to be forced into acquiescence rather than petitioned for help, and those in special contact with the unseen world were medicine-men (*shamans*) whose magic powers came in trance. Even marriage was dramatized as warfare, and even bereavement called for the destruction of property and perhaps the killing of some other person. Through everything there ran this thread of vainglory, this desire to dominate others, this flaunting competitiveness, in the never-ending pursuit of prestige.

---

1. See *Patterns of Culture,* by Ruth Benedict (Routledge, London, 1935 and Mifflin, Boston, 1934).

How different the life of the Pueblo, where mildness is all! Today there dwell on the arid wastes of New Mexico the Pueblo Indians, past their peak days of great valley cities of stone, but still leading a well integrated life of ceremonious sobriety. In their villages anger is *tabu* on all ritual occasions, and daily life is sober and kindly and inoffensive. No great display is made of wealth, no great store set by the exclusive possession of private property, no great urge felt for personal power and authority. In marriage and divorce passionate feelings are not paraded nor violent jealousy displayed; children grow up without terrible ordeals of initiation and without deep resentments requiring urgent outlet; the unavoidable pains of bereavement are mollified and not flaunted. Deeply absorbed in religious ritual, the Pueblo Indian obtains his supernatural prerogatives by membership of a group and by acquisition of magic formulae, not by an ecstatic experience dependent on drugs or self-torture or cataleptic trance. His ritual dances are meticulously repetitive but not frenzied, his fasting a means of ritual cleansing but not of exaltation, his religious officials priests but not *shamans.* Disruptive experiences of all sorts are avoided, excesses of all kinds disapproved. Pueblo life is the life of the golden mean.

The conclusion is clear. Two groups of Amerindians, biologically very similar, developed temperaments and social institutions and behaviour patterns poles apart. From the vast array of cultural traits of which human nature is capable, each people comes to value a limited selection—just as it uses in its speech only a small number of the voice-sounds which the human mouth can make. Within any one society, there may be some individuals whose innate temperamental tendencies are not congenial with the dominant behaviour pattern, and they are the social misfits who may become mentally ill; but so plastic is human nature that most members of any society adopt without too much discomfort whatever values and attitudes and activities that society ordains. There is no biological reason to suppose that the innate potentialities of Kwakiutl and Pueblo Indians are appreciably different, yet their learned behaviours could scarcely be less similar. And, seeing in this case how contrasted are the characters of two peoples so close in ancestry, we should do well to demand firm proof before accepting any statement that this or that personality characteristic is innate in one or another so-called 'race'. Human genetical variation is sufficiently striking, but the variation in character according to cultural conditioning is more striking still.

7. The History of Population Mixture

Part of the current confusion of thought on the matter of race is due to the misleading nature of the common comparison of the process of evolution to the branching of a tree. 'The tree of life' is thought of as having many main branches, one of which is the mammals; and this mammalian branch is thought of as having produced smaller and smaller branches, one of these being *Homo sapiens*. Then, by an extension of the analogy, the human branch is visualized as having four or five branchlets, each of which is a so-called 'race'. It is important that the teacher should clear his pupils' minds of this entirely misleading visualization. The formation of human ethnic groups is not, in fact, at all well represented by the analogy of the branching of a tree. If a visual analogy is wanted, a better one would be that of a fisherman's net or a piece of wire netting, in which the individual strands repeatedly come together here and move apart there. Even this, however, does not fully represent the complexity of the situation, for the process of population segregation and admixture is one which has gone on irregularly and intermittently during long ages and in which many ethnic groups of all sorts and sizes have participated. Thus, the only model which would do anything like justice to the facts would be a very complex one in three dimensions.

At the top of the model, picturing the position today, there would be a strand for each individual now alive, and these strands would be clustered together in small groups representing families. These small clusters would be grouped in rather larger clusters representing local interbreeding populations, and these in yet larger clusters representing wider but still related populations. And so it would go on, clusters of clusters of clusters, culminating in a few major clusters representing the four or five main ethnic groups. But everywhere strands would be seen criss-crossing from one cluster to another, and the closer one looked the less sharply would one be able to separate this cluster from that. At the bottom of the model, picturing the position in the early days of man's history, there would not be nearly so many strands, for the world's population was then far smaller; and the clusters would be less definite than at the top of the model, for the main differentiation of ethnic groups had not yet occurred. Moving up the model from its base as the long ages of prehistory pass by, the strands would become grouped in closer clusters during periods in which populations were isolated; and, for some distance up, there would be only an occasional strand connecting one cluster with another. Then, as the isolating factors of climate or geography or social barriers were modified or overcome, the connecting strands would increase in number; and, in places, one cluster or another would almost disappear. Yet higher up the model, there might be other periods of sharply defined clusters, but these clusters would not be identical with those lower down or those higher up. 'Races' were formed, 'races' were dissolved, old 'races' being ever modified and new 'races' being ever in the process of formation. But always the so-called 'race' is a mere cluster of individual strands, and it is ever the individual which is the unit of reality.

The fact is, not only are there no 'pure' races today, but there never have been. From the very start of man's history, when ethnic group variations were first developing, admixture has been going on. As a result, even the three great groups of Negroids, Mongoloids and Caucasoids cannot be distinguished sharply. From Africa to Asia a line can be traced along which the populations become progressively less Negroid and more Mongoloid, from Europe to Africa a line along which Negroid characteristics gradually replace Caucasoid, from Europe to Asia a line along which the people grade from Caucasoid to Mongoloid. There have in the past been periods of comparatively little mixture, but never, so far as we know, has the isolation been long or complete enough to allow the formation of 'pure races'. Always there has been some intermixture, and in some historical periods (including our own) a great deal of it, and so the common pool of humanity's hereditary genes has been kept stirred up. Nor is there any reason to suppose that this miscegenation through the ages has been at all harmful.[1]

A good example of interbreeding is found in the Norfolk and Pitcairn Islands, whose exceptionally healthy inhabitants are the descendants of nine English sailors (who mutinied on the *Bounty* in 1789) and the Tahitian women whom they took with them to Pitcairn. Throughout Polynesia, miscegenation has been proceeding for the past couple of centuries, and has produced a population entirely harmonious in physical and mental characteristics. The Seminole Indians of Oklahoma, descendants of three-way crossing between American Whites, Negroes and Creek Indians, show no evidence of degeneration due to population crossing. In the U.S.A., in Jamaica, and elsewhere, the offspring of Negro-White crossing is producing intermediate types in no way biologically inferior to the parental types; and the same applies to the crossing of Malayan and European, of Dutch and Hottentot, of Bushman and Basuto and Kaffir and Zulu. The risks of interbreeding are scarcely at all biological, but almost exclusively social in nature—and social disadvantages are not necessary if we determine to dispel them.

Many schools today include in the history syllabus a broad-sweeping account of the world's great population movements, and this makes it possible to give children a realistic if

---

1. For further evidence on this point, see *Man's Most Dangerous Myth: the Fallacy of Race*, by M. F. Ashley Montagu (Columbia University Press, New York, 1952, third edition).

elementary understanding of the ethnic complexity of modern populations. There are few traces in Europe today of the apparently Negroid and Mongoloid peoples whose fossilized bones betray their presence in palaeolithic times, but there are ample signs of the repeated incursions into Europe of different 'pink' or Caucasoid peoples. Some came via the Ukraine into the northern lands, others up the Danube into the central regions, others along the narrow shores of North Africa and into the Iberian peninsula, yet others by sea to the Mediterranean and Atlantic coastal regions—mingling and again mingling, leaving Europe with an ethnic map of kaleidoscopic confusion.[1]

In Greece, and wherever Greece's glories grace the school curriculum, children may learn how Hellenism emerged from a people who interbred freely with invaders of various stocks; in Italy, and wherever the Roman genius has left its mark in literature or law, children may learn how the Latin culture came from a people of ethnically mixed origins. Across the world, wherever the British have settled, children should know that they are the product of innumerable crossings between the aboriginal Britons and successive waves of invaders —Roman, Saxon, Jute, Danish, Norwegian, Norman—to say nothing of the absorption of miscellaneous groups of Scots, Irish, French, German, Italian, Spanish and so on. France has seen the fusion of various population groups, Germany is rich not only in Nordic but also in Alpine and Slavonic elements, and so the tale might continue. Scarcely a land could be found in which the centuries have not seen the same continuous mixing of genetic ingredients which we can observe going on in America and elsewhere today. The evidence is overwhelming that miscegenation provides no necessary hindrance to cultural richness.

We have not got such detailed knowledge of population movements and ethnic mixture outside Europe, but it is clear that the general picture is similar. In India the population ranges in skin colour from very pale to very dark, and

1. For details, see *We Europeans,* by J. S. Huxley, A. C. Haddon and A. M. Carr-Saunders (Penguin, London, 1939).

represents the result of admixture, in varying degrees in the various castes and the different geographical regions, between the aboriginal inhabitants and successive waves of immigrants. In Central Asia there has been admixture between Causasoids and Mongoloids of many different types; in the Sudan a miscellany of Negroid and Caucasoid peoples have interbred; in Polynesia the people are patently of mixed Caucasoid, Mongoloid and Negroid ancestry. Everywhere there has been miscegenation, and everywhere these mixed populations have been able to produce civilizations appropriate to their material conditions of life. And, a particularly striking example, the complex anthropological character of the Jewish people has derived from many movements and mixings of populations and has been accompanied by a peculiarly rich cultural achievement.

Nor are these processes of population mingling and population differentiation at an end. The 'Cape Coloureds' of South Africa are the product of comparatively recent miscegenation between European settlers and natives, and constitute a recognizable ethnic group. Similarly in Brazil, there is gradually emerging a new ethnic type based on the miscegenation of aboriginal Amerindians, the descendants of imported African slaves, and European settlers; while in Hawaii there is proceeding a large-scale admixture of native Hawaiians, Chinese, Polynesians and Europeans. Population mingling and differentiation go on today, as they have gone on in the past and will continue in the future. The admixture of ethnic groups is not a temporary or exceptional phenomenon: it is of the very essence of the human species.

Teachers are familiar with the way in which a class of intelligent children will follow up, often in a quite unexpected direction, the implications of some point in a lesson. They will not, therefore, be surprised if discussions on intermarriage arise with their pupils in a wide range of situations. The matter may come up directly in biology lessons when heredity or evolution are being dealt with, or it may arise in connexion with geography or history or social studies. In some schools religious instruction will also raise the point, and in others the matter may arise in connexion with the plot of a novel or a play. The teacher's task is sometimes relatively easy: he has only to expound the simple biological facts, indicating that there is no reason to expect the offspring of mixed marriages to be in any biological way inferior to those of ethnically similar parents. In other places, local conditions may make it desirable for the teacher to point out that, quite apart from the biological results of miscegenation, there may be social and cultural handicaps making it very difficult for the children so born to get a fair start in life. In yet other places, where there is not merely prejudice against mixed marriages but actual legal prohibition of them, the task of the teacher who wishes to deal with the facts honestly may be difficult in the extreme. But, although the teacher must decide in the light of local circumstances just how he will deal with the facts, about the facts themselves there is little room for dispute.

8. The Ideology of Human Equality

There still exist, in backward regions of the world, remnants of primitive religions which draw a sharp distinction between the respective human value of members of the tribe and of those outside it; and, regrettably, there still remain in the technically advanced areas those who share the Nazi doctrine of the innate superiority of a particular ethnic group. But most of the great religions of the world are universalist in nature, and so are the declared ideologies of nearly all the major nations. True, deed does not always match up to word, and many men act in ways contrary to the spirit of their religious faith and political affiliation; but this does not alter the great central fact, which is that the consensus of considered human thought deplores and opposes all types of racial prejudice and discrimination. Nor should the teacher hesitate to impress this fact, for fact it is, upon his pupils. He will need to use tact and discretion; but he should not allow fear of offending the prejudiced to stand in the way of his plain duty to proclaim the truth.

Naturally, the teacher will do nothing to diminish the very proper pride of children in their own ethnic group. The Caucasoid peoples generally may be reasonably proud of the material and cultural benefits which they have brought to wide areas of the earth, Negroids may very naturally take pride in the enormous advances in culture which they have achieved in a comparatively short period of time, Mongoloids may look back proudly to their ancient civilizations and forward to their doubtless great future. Similarly, national and religious groups may be expected to foster regard for their own special features; but all this can be done without any assumption of innate superiority or any contempt for groups to which one does not happen to belong.

Both Jews and Christians teach their children, sometimes at home and sometimes at school, about the early history of the Hebrew people as portrayed in the Old Testament. Both, therefore, should ensure that their children read these ancient scriptures intelligently, as the expression of the emergence of a great spiritual conception and not as a collection of texts to be uncritically quoted. And, wherever Jews and Christians share in a society, it would be an excellent idea to give an objective account of their different interpretations of the common Holy Writ. When the schoolchild reads, in the Book of Genesis, 'Cursed be Canaan; a servant of servants shall he be unto his brethren', or when he reads Isaac's injunction to Jacob, 'Thou shalt not take a wife of the daughters of Canaan', he might take such passages as indicating an intolerant racial exclusiveness on the part of the Jews; in fact, however, the Jews distinguished themselves from their neighbours by theological rather than biological differences. In any event, the Old Testament contains many universalist sentiments and aspirations, as where Isaiah foresees the day when 'the Lord of hosts shall bless, saying, Blessed be Egypt my people, and Assyria the work of my hand, and Israel my inheritance', or where he prophesies 'it shall come, that I will gather all nations and tongues'. The whole of the tenth chapter of Genesis, with its attempt at a total genealogy of the world's peoples, is a particularly striking example of early Jewish universalism. And, when the teacher is discussing with his pupils the story of Adam and Eve, he would be in the company of many theologians in taking this tale as a symbol of the essential unity of all mankind.

Despite the racialism of the so-called 'German Christians' under Hitler, despite the racialism which has crept into certain churches and sects from time to time, the central Christian faith proclaims unambiguously the essential unity of mankind and the intrinsic human dignity of each individual. Thus, in schools in which there is Christian religious education, the situation is very favourable for the combating of racial prejudice. The idea of 'God the Father' implies that all men are brothers, and the fact that at some times and in some places the Christian Church has tolerated racial discrimination can in no way obscure this central belief. Indeed, it might be a good thing if, where a school exhibits images of the Godhead, the face depicted were sometimes of Negroid or Mongoloid type, instead of the more usual Western European 'pale face'. Certainly, if this were done, the children would be prompted to ask questions which the teacher could answer in a most illuminating manner.

In the New Testament, there are many passages which clearly condemn ethnic discrimination and assert the brotherhood of man. St. Paul, in his Epistle to the Ephesians, affirmed that 'There is neither Jew nor Greek'; in St. John's Gospel the Jews were told that Jesus died 'not for that nation only, but that also he should gather together in one the children of God that were scattered abroad'; in the Revelation of St. John the Divine we read not of a particular 'race' but of 'a great multitude, which no man could number, of all nations, and kindreds, and people, and tongues'. St. Luke tells us how, when a lawyer asked 'And who is my neighbour?', Jesus replied with the parable of the good Samaritan, a man of a despised ethnic group, who cut straight through the Jewish-Samaritan barrier in a simple act of human kindness. It is perhaps a perilous thing to make any statement about what Jesus would do if he were alive today, but all that we know of his life gives support to the view that he would mix with whatever people suffer from racial discrimination. It is interesting also to note that the Koran recognizes liberty of conscience and that Mohammed urged Mohammedans to live in peace with Christians and Jews. And, despite the conflicts between Moslems and Hindus which preceded and accompanied the partition of India, the more responsible leaders of both religions deplore this pseudo-racial tension as contrary to the best theological thought.

In schools which give Christian instruction or which exist in a cultural environment shaped by Christian beliefs, it is important that the New Testament story should not be allowed to encourage the growth of anti-Semitic feeling. It is by no means unknown for Christian children to develop antipathy towards the Jews because 'they crucified Jesus'—as if one were to condemn all Greeks because 'they killed Socrates', or all English because 'they killed Joan of Arc'. Even where the facts are not distorted in this way, and no blame is imputed to the Jewish people as a whole, it often happens that the fact that Jesus also was a Jew is glossed over. Yet, the emergence of the new religion of Christianity cannot be properly appreciated except in its essentially Jewish historical context, and we cannot expect Christian children to understand their own religion unless they have a sympathetic understanding of Judaism. The religious genius of Israel lies at the very heart of Christianity: to present Jesus as in opposition to the Jews is not only to encourage Jewish-Gentile tension but also to misrepresent the facts, while to present him as a Jew of the Jews is not only to respect historical truth but also to encourage charity and toleration. Mary and Joseph were Jews and so were the twelve apostles: if children were more *vividly* aware of such facts, they might be less inclined to harbour anti-Semitic sentiments.

However, it is not only in religious instruction that the teacher has the opportunity of encouraging in his pupils a civilized attitude towards people of different ethnic groups. Any study of the history of art, or of science, or of human thought in general, will bring to the pupils' notice examples of the important cultural contributions of individuals of many different nations and faiths and ancestries. Every secondary school, moreover, includes in its curriculum various historical and geographical studies which cannot be adequately dealt with unless the nettle of racial prejudice is firmly grasped. For example, the history of the expansion of British power in Africa and America does not make sense without reference to the treatment of the natives of those two continents and to the slave trade by which the forebears of the modern American Negroes were transferred across the ocean; and it would be a rare group of pupils which could not profitably discuss the morality of these matters. Similarly, children may learn about Australia's restrictions on Asiatic immigrants, about French anti-Semitism in the Dreyfus case, about the way in which the Czarist régime instigated pogroms of the Jews to divert the attention of the peasants and city workers from their bad living conditions.

Then, to turn to the more favourable side of the medal, they may learn how New Zealand has now established civilized relations between its Pakehas (citizens of European descent) and its Maoris, how in West Africa and the Gold Coast the native inhabitants have moved towards self-government, and how in the U.S.A. wide cracks are appearing in the colour-bar. These topics are not unwarranted intrusions into history and geography: they are an essential part of it. Without the life-blood of such human relations, history is only chronology and geography is mere topography.

When the teacher of geography is considering with his class the Union of South Africa, a country where a minority of 'Europeans' exercises hegemony over a majority of 'Africans' and 'Coloureds' and 'Indians', his pupils may well question the justice of this state of affairs, especially if they know that Queen Victoria's proclamation annexing Natal in 1843 included the assurance that there would be no discrimination 'on mere distinction of colour, origin, language or creed'. And, while the teacher must recognize the quite real social problems of such a polyethnic community and the honestly held convictions of many of the 'Europeans', he is entitled—indeed, he is morally bound—also to put the arguments for racial tolerance. Moreover, although the 'white' Christians of Africa have rarely admitted the natives of that continent to full fellowship, in recent years there have been declarations against racial discrimination by the Protestant Christian Council of South Africa and by the Roman Catholic Archbishop and Bishops of that land.[1] Further, the general biological, sociological and humanist arguments adduced elsewhere in this booklet are very relevant to any classroom discussion of the human geography of South Africa.

Similarly, the United States of America, where there are not only millions of Negroes and some surviving Amerindians but also various other minority groups such as Chinese and Japanese and Puerto Ricans and Mexicans, afford great possibilities for the study of race relations. In the U.S.A., as in South Africa, racial segregation has developed even within the churches, and as long ago as 1891 the Archbishop of St. Paul remarked that 'slavery has been abolished in America; the trail of the serpent, however, yet marks the ground'. He went on to ask, 'What do I claim for the black man?' and replied, 'That which I claim for the white man, neither more nor less. I would blot out the colour line.' During recent years, the Churches of America have come to see that segregation is inconsistent with Christianity, and progress is being made in the integration of congregations of different colours.

Although the American Declaration of Independence contains a derogatory reference to 'the merciless Indian Savages', and although some of its early proponents held no brief for the Negro, nevertheless that Declaration includes the unequivocal statement that 'We hold these truths to be self-evident, that all men are created equal . . .' More specifically, the Fifteenth Amendment to the U.S. Constitution declares that 'The right of citizens of the United States to vote shall not be denied or abridged by the United States or by any State on account of race, colour, or previous condition of servitude.' In some Southern states of the U.S.A., the teacher is on very delicate

1. The Christian attitude to race is discussed in the Unesco pamphlets *The Catholic Church and the Race Question,* by Father Congar (Paris, 1953) and *The Ecumenical Movement and the Racial Problem,* by W. A. Visser't Hooft (Paris, 1954).

ground in dealing with the question of colour discrimination, but these constitutional declarations provide a clear statement of the legal basis for non-discrimination. In order to show how progress in this matter has been achieved mention might also be made of the three great Presidential Commissions set up since the end of the Second World War. The Committee on Civil Rights declared roundly in 1947 that 'democracy . . . means that in going to school, working, participating in the political process, serving in the armed forces, enjoying government services in such fields as health and recreation, making use of transportation and other public accommodation facilities, and living in specific communities, distinctions of race, colour, and creed have no place'. Similarly, the Commission on Higher Education has called for the end of all segregation in universities and colleges, and the Committee on Equality of Treatment and Opportunity in the Armed Services has made a similar demand (now very largely met) for the abolition of all racial discrimination in the military forces of the U.S.A. And, finally, a series of Supreme Court judgements has increasingly liberated Negroes from segregation in public vehicles, housing schemes and educational institutions.

Questions of racial relations also arise in any consideration of the geography of the British Commonwealth of Nations. Although in England itself the overwhelming majority of the people are 'pink', in the Commonwealth as a whole the 'pinks' are in a small minority. And, although most English children rarely come into contact with people of African or Asian ancestry, in London and the great seaports a classroom may have 'white', 'black', 'brown' and 'yellow' children sitting amicably side by side. However, it often happens that during adolescence colour prejudice becomes more acute, and sometimes there is tension when unemployment rears its ugly head and adults of different colours are in competition for jobs. The general atmosphere in Britain is favourable to the development of civilized racial attitudes; but a certain rather subtle colour prejudice may create difficulties for Negroes and Indians (in most cases not foreigners but fellow-citizens of the British Commonwealth), in regard, for example, to housing. And since, apart from a few thousand university students, most of the coloured men in Britain are seafarers and unskilled workers, there has developed a certain correlation between colour and social status, so that a dark skin may tend to be regarded as socially if not ethnically inferior. This does not prevent Negroes and Indians from practising medicine in a mainly 'white' neighbourhood or from teaching in schools all of whose children are 'white', but prejudice and discrimination are by no means entirely absent from England.[1] In other parts of the Commonwealth the situation is a good deal sharper, and the Mau-Mau troubles in Kenya are but one indication of the difficulties that may lie ahead. The long period of white supremacy is ending, and now the teachers of emergent Africa and Asia will have to guard against the development in their pupils of a compensating anti-White racialism.

Just as the Constitution of the U.S.A. and the Common Law of England make no distinction between citizens on grounds of ethnic origin, neither do the modern constitutions of most other major countries. Thus, the Preamble to the French Constitution 'proclaims anew that every human being, without distinction of race, religion or creed, possesses inalienable and sacred rights', and in France there is remarkably little strong colour prejudice. In Germany, despite the shameful history of anti-Semitism under the Nazis, the teacher can point with pride to the brave defiance of Christian leaders like Pastor Niemoller and Bishop Wurm of Wurtemburg, and can quote the postwar declaration of the Synod of the Evangelical Church admitting 'that by negligence and silence we became accessory . . . to the crime committed against the Jews' and proclaiming the 'spirit of brotherhood' anew.

As another example from Europe, we may take the Sixty-ninth Article of the Polish Constitution: 'Citizens of the Polish People's Republic, irrespective of nationality, race or religion enjoy equal rights in all spheres of public, political, economic, social and cultural life. Infringement of this principle by any

1. A careful study of the situation is presented in *Negroes in Britain: A Study of Racial Relations in English Society*, by K. L. Little (Kegan Paul, London, 1948).

direct or indirect granting of privileges or restriction of rights, on account of nationality, race or religion, is punishable by law. The spreading of hatred or contempt, the provocation of strife or the humiliation of man on account of national, racial or religious differences are forbidden.' Or, if we care to cross to the other side of the globe, we shall find similar principles enunciated in the Constitution of the People's Republic of China: 'All component racial groups in the Republic of China shall enjoy equal rights' (Chapter I, Article 5) and 'All citizens of the Republic of China, irrespective of sex, religion, race, class or party affiliation, shall be equal before the law' (Chapter II, Article 7).

In the U.S.S.R., also, the Constitution is quite explicit on the matter of race: 'Equality of rights of citizens of the U.S.S.R., irrespective of their nationality or race, in all spheres of economic, government, cultural, political and other public activity, is an indefeasible law. Any direct or indirect restriction of the rights of, or conversely, the establishment of any direct or indirect privileges for, citizens on account of their race or nationality, as well as any advocacy of racial or national exclusiveness or of hatred and contempt, is punishable by law' (Article 123). In Russia, as elsewhere, constitutional guarantees have not always been matched by actual practice, and certainly there have been cases of anti-Semitism from time to time. Nevertheless, in this vast land where pogroms of the Jews were formerly notorious, racial discrimination is recognized in the constitution to be wrong and punishable by law.

Finally, we may note the Universal Declaration of Human Rights;[1] adopted by the main nations of the world on 10 December 1948:

'*Article 1*. All human beings are born free and equal in dignity and rights. They are endowed with reason and conscience and should act towards one another in a spirit of brotherhood.

---

1. The full text of the Declaration, with an account of its origins and suggestions for its educational use, is given in *The Universal Declaration of Human Rights: A Guide for Teachers*, published by Unesco (Paris, 1953).

'*Article 2*. Everyone is entitled to all the rights and freedoms set forth in this Declaration, without distinction of any kind, such as race, colour, sex, language, religion, political or other opinion, national or social origin, property, birth or other status. . . .

'*Article 16*. (1) Men and women of full age, without any limitation due to race, nationality or religion have the right to marry and to found a family. . . .

'*Article 27*. (1) Everyone has the right freely to participate in the cultural life of the community. . . .'

Thus, wherever the teacher looks, to the great world religions or to the major philosophies of history, to the constitutions of the great powers or to the declarations of the United Nations, to the manifestos of men of goodwill whatever their political affiliations, he sees the same vision. That vision is of a world in which all men are equal in human value, in which ethnic origin is an irrelevance in considering political and social rights. It is the vision which we want our pupils to share.

9. The Growth of Racial Prejudice

The intelligent pupil, faced with the testimony to human unity given by the great religions and great philosophers, will naturally wonder why in the past there has been so much racial intolerance. And, learning that most of the chief nations and the chief international organizations assert the equal rights of all ethnic groups, he will wonder why still today there is so much racial discrimination. It is, of course, no novelty for children to discover discrepancies between adult principle and adult practice; and the danger is that they may very easily come to accept such discrepancies as a sign of adult status. The teacher knows how easy it is for children to keep in separate compartments of their personalities what they learn in school and what they learn at home or from the world outside, and it is one of the most important of the teacher's tasks to try to prevent such separation.

If what we teach our pupils about race is to have an outcome not only in knowledge but also in behaviour, if it is to produce more than mere verbal idealism, we have to make them vividly aware of the ways in which the whole issue has in the past been bedevilled by economic and imperialist self-interest and is today befogged by intellectual dishonesty and emotional confusion. In some schools there may be occasional discussions specifically designed to deal with this matter, in other schools there may be repeated reference whenever relevant in courses in history and geography and social studies; but, whatever the mode of approach, the teacher will need to be familiar with the facts. And the most striking fact is that racial prejudice is not inherent in the nature of humanity but emerges and gathers strength only in certain social conditions. It is, of course, a common observation that members of any 'in-group' tend to be prejudiced against the members of an 'out-group'—conquerors against conquered, old residents against newcomers, one neighbouring tribe against another—but this does not mean that intergroup tensions are unavoidable. It is also a fact that colour prejudice may be exhibited by those whose skins are yellow or brown or black, as well as by those whose skins are white, but this does not mean that colour prejudice is innate. Indeed, infants of different religions and different colours will commonly play unselfconsciously together, only learning prejudice gradually from their elders.

Early Greek society was based in part on the servitude of a subject group, but this was a matter of military conquest rather than of any theory of 'racial' inferiority; in ancient Rome, political and social rights went with citizenship, not with skin colour. In India, it is true, the caste system developed with a correlation between status and pigmentation—indeed, the Sanskrit word for caste is *varna*, meaning 'colour', but this seems to have been an almost accidental outcome of the fact that the conquerors were of paler hue than the conquered. In early Christendom, the great gulf was between the faithful and the non-believers, and ethnic origin was irrelevant; the great new force of Mohammedanism recognized no essential distinction between black and brown and white, but only between those who embraced Islam and those who did not. Naturally, people in those days were quite well aware that individuals differed in colour and hair texture and facial features, and they recognized that sometimes those physical differences were correlated with differences in cultural level, but a man was not condemned to social segregation or political impotence because he was of a different so-called 'race'. In those early days there was cruelty and religious intolerance and economic exploitation, but there was usually little of the colour prejudice which we know in the world today.

In Africa Negroes enslaved Negroes, in India the paler-skinned high castes discriminated against the darker-skinned low castes, but it was not until the fifteenth and sixteenth centuries that an ideology specifically justifying racial discrimination really began to gain ground. The great Iberian and British mariners opened up the ocean routes of the world, and for the first time the technically advanced Europeans had the opportunity to dominate darker-skinned peoples on a large scale. In the common way of conquerors and colonists, seeking rich plunder and cheap labour for their new estates, the Spanish and Portuguese *conquistadores* exploited the natives of Central and South America quite flagrantly. And, since among them were men no more heartless than the rest of mankind, who took seriously the Christian teaching that all men are brothers, there were vehement protests at this cruel treatment. Disturbed consciences had to be stilled, and the fable was fabricated that the Amerindians were inferior, scarcely human, creatures to whom the brotherhood of man did not extend.

Part of the difficulty was that in many respects the European conquerors were in fact superior: Cortés managed to take over the empire of Mexico with a mere six hundred Spaniards, and Pizarro conquered Peru with an even smaller army.

It is common enough for the victor to be contemptuous of the vanquished—the Normans despised the English after the Battle of Hastings—and it takes a person of some perspicacity to distinguish between cultural or technical inadequacy and innate inferiority. And, of course, when self-interest so demands, the distinction tends to be not only obscured but almost wilfully avoided. Thus, in 1550, Juan Ginés de Sepúlveda asserted[1] that 'Indians are as different from Spaniards as cruelty is from kindness and monkeys are from men', and such views were welcome to many who had an economic stake in the exploitation of the new lands.

But not all allowed profits to suppress principles, and there were admirable priests, like Fray Bartolomé de Las Casas, who worked unwearyingly for the proposition that all people are of equal value as human beings. Similarly Pope Paul III, in a series of Bulls on the race question, opposed as the work of the devil 'the opinion that the inhabitants of the West Indies and the southern continents, of whose existence we have but recently learnt, should be treated like animals that have not reason, and be employed solely for our profit and our service, on the pretext that they have no part in the Catholic faith and are incapable of adopting it'. In France at this same time we find Montaigne (1533-92) proclaiming of the native Brazilians that 'There is nothing savage or barbarian about this nation save for the fact that each of us labels whatever is not among the customs of his own peoples as barbarous'; and through the next two centuries other French thinkers, such as Voltaire (1694-1778) and Rousseau (1712-78), were determined supporters of the concept of human unity.

Unfortunately, the biological work of Buffon (1707-88) and the anthropological studies of Blumenbach (1752-1840) helped to direct attention to the differences between various human groups, and their scientific generalizations were widely misrepresented and distorted. In the event, the great truths of science and theology and philosophy were no match for

1. See *Racial Myths,* by Juan Comas, published by Unesco (Paris, 1951).

the mighty forces of economic exploitation, and the idea of innate racial inferiority entered insidiously into European thought. When teachers of history are dealing with this period, they can give their teaching additional life by outlining for their pupils this conflict between human charity and toleration on the one hand, and human avarice and self-delusion on the other.

England had been involved in the slave trade ever since 1562, when Hawkins carried his first cargo of 'black flesh' to San Domingo and established a mutually profitable connexion with the Spanish settlers; but forty years later colour prejudice was still so slight that Shakespeare's Othello married Desdemona. However, by the end of the seventeenth century, the English colonists in Virginia and the East Indies were also taking in slave labour on a large scale, and in 1712 the Treaty of Utrecht gave Britain a monopoly of the slave trade with the Spanish colonies. The eighteenth century saw marked mechanical improvement in Lancashire's mills, and the voracious appetite of 'King Cotton' demanded ever new supplies of raw material. To meet this demand, the great cotton-growing areas of America required more and more plantation workers; and this need was met partly by the direct importing of further Negro slaves and partly by the offspring of those already in America. It is difficult to estimate the sum of human suffering involved in the trade of slavery and its inevitable concomitants.

It is important to remember, however, that throughout the eighteenth century many men, women and children of England itself were being kidnapped and sold abroad into indentured labour; and the slave trade, while a clear sign of callousness, did not necessarily imply racial discrimination. Indeed, although the elegant ladies and gentlemen of England indulged from about 1650 in the fashionable whim of keeping 'blackamoor' (and later, Chinese) pages and personal servants, they not infrequently educated them and knew that Negroes were quite capable of culture. The sons of African chiefs were being sent to England for their education and received as 'Black Gentlemen' in high social circles, and a few Negroes of intellectual distinction were mixing on equal terms with white-skinned men of letters. Thus, at this time, the fact that most Negroes in England occupied menial posts had no necessary implication of ethnic inferiority: rather, it was one facet of a society in which those who wielded power were as ready to keep 'Whites' as to keep 'Blacks' in subjection.

Many of the literary figures of eighteenth-century England —Steele, Pope, Sterne, Johnson—protested against slavery and some were definitely negrophile. There was a widespread feeling that 'the air of England is free', and during the 1760s and 1770s a series of test cases in the Courts eventually established the legal freedom on English soil of former slaves. Humanitarian effort was continued by Wilberforce and others, and in 1807 Britain prohibited the slave trade. By 1834 slavery was made illegal throughout the British Empire, in 1843 France followed suit, and in 1863 the Dutch government did likewise.

Unfortunately, as the Negroes of the U.S.A. were to discover again nearly a century later, the legal abolition of slavery did not solve all problems. In 1770 there were probably some 15,000 Negroes in London, mostly slaves but usually fairly well cared for; by 1780 the streets of the city were trod by hundreds of Negro beggars, free but destitute. Several hundred sailed in 1786, transported and fed at government expense, to found Freetown in Sierra Leone, but this only touched the fringe of the problem. The majority found some employment as coachmen, footmen, Army bandsmen, seamen, pedlars and unskilled workers of many sorts, while some few succeeded as independent traders. But, now that they were free, Negroes were no longer a focus of humanitarian effort, and it is even possible that the pity which they had earlier evoked left an aftermath of condescension. Moreover, the opening up of Africa revealed great groups of people who were both heathen and heavily pigmented, and it was natural enough that white skins tended increasingly to be equated with civilized Christianity and black skins with primitive paganism. As the novels of Thackeray and others show, there was emerging in the early decades of the nineteenth century a quite specific colour prejudice, and as the years went by this became much more marked.

In earlier days, the apologists of slavery and white domination produced Biblical arguments based on 'the curse of Canaan' or simply asserted that Negroes were innately inferior and fit for nothing better; now, in the latter half of the nineteenth century, they were provided with a new pseudo-scientific armament. Misapplying Darwin's theory of evolution by natural selection, many Europeans asserted that, since the 'Whites' were manifestly doing better than the 'Blacks' in the struggle for existence, the former were the 'fittest' group of mankind and the latter an inferior group—a peculiarly blatant distortion of biology of which the science teacher should certainly disabuse his pupils' minds. And even the devoted efforts of missionaries, by drawing attention to the degraded state of many Africans, reinforced in European minds the idea that Negroes constituted an inferior group of mankind. In 1885, the Berlin Conference carved up Africa among the powers of Europe, and qualms of conscience were fairly easily stilled by talk of 'the white man's burden'. When the history of these times is being taught at school, the teacher has an excellent opportunity to help in eradicating racial prejudice.

Similarly, when the teacher is dealing with the history of America, it is quite impossible for him to escape the issue of slavery or the arguments about innate ethnic differences involved in it. There has been much careful and scholarly study of the history of slavery and the complex pattern of Negro-White relations in the U.S.A., and the teacher should have no difficulty in finding adequate source material for his lessons.[1] Even during the eighteenth century there were many Americans, especially among the Quakers and Evangelicals, who opposed slavery; but the great turning point was the war between the North and the slave-holding South.

---

1. See *Documents Illustrative of the History of the Slave Trade to America*, by Elizabeth Donnan (Carnegie Institute of Washington, 1930); *The Negro's Struggle for Survival*, by S. J. Holmes (University of California Press, 1937); and periodicals such as *Phylon: a Review of Race and Culture* (Atlanta University, Georgia). The recent period is dealt with in *Negro Status and Race Relations in the United States: 1911-1946* (Phelps-Stokes Fund, New York, 1948).

Following the Civil War came the brief Reconstruction period, when emancipated 'Black' and 'poor White' combined in an effort to govern the areas in which they lived. This was a time when passions ran high, when the brief hope of brotherhood in the Southern states burned brightly before it was extinguished by violence and counter-violence. Those were the days when the Ku Klux Klan lit the fiery cross, and left embers that still smoulder sullenly in some places to this day.

Before many years had passed, in a South still built on cotton, the political disfranchisement of the Negroes was accomplished by a variety of devices, and racial segregation became firmly established. In this atmosphere the mythology of racial inferiority proliferated, those who suggested that men of all colours should be treated equally were liable to be regarded as cranks or worse, and quite kind men and women became the victims of their own prejudices. Even organized Christianity practised segregation, and to this day most American Negroes worship in separate churches or separate congregations. But, today, American society is changing rapidly: the market for U.S. cotton and tobacco has been partially captured by other lands, industry is developing in the South, increasing mobility is releasing Southerners from regional isolation, unsegregated service in the armed forces has opened the eyes of many young Americans both 'Black' and 'White', U.S. Supreme Court rulings are helping to break down discrimination in travel and in education, the Churches are recognizing the evil of segregation in worship, the political parties are eagerly seeking the Negro vote, and up and down the land civil rights associations are fighting racial discrimination. All this is the very stuff of the contemporary American scene, and school teaching which ignores it is out of touch with reality.

In Europe, the more characteristic expression of group intolerance is not the colour-bar but anti-Semitism. All children who read the Old Testament will know that the early Jews had their own homeland Israel, but few have any appreciable knowledge of the subsequent history of this long-wandering people. From quite early times there were Jewish settlements in the cities of the Greek and Roman worlds, but it was shortly after the beginning of the Christian era that the main dispersion occurred. Conquered like so many other nations by the Romans, and like other nations desiring independence, the Jewish people repeatedly rebelled against their imperial masters. Eventually, the Roman retribution was ruthless: the Jews found their towns and villages destroyed and their land laid desolate, and they made their way wherever they might settle. Here and there they were persecuted—in pagan Rome, Christian and Jew were cast into the arena side by side since neither would admit the divinity of the emperor—but, generally speaking, for some centuries the Jews pursued their lives and made their devotions at peace with their pagan and Christian neighbours.

In the seventh century, the emergence of Islam introduced a new factor. Finding the Jews unwilling to accept his religious claims, Mohammed destroyed several of their communities in his native Arabia; but, later, the monotheistic Jews and the Christians were tolerated as 'People of the Book'. In A.D. 638 the Caliph Omar reopened Jerusalem (captured from Byzantium) to the Jews, and new Jewish settlements followed the expanding Moslem power. There were setbacks—under the great Harun al-Rashid both Jews and Christians suffered various restrictions and in A.D. 850 the Jews were compelled to wear a yellow patch on their clothing—but by the tenth century the Jewish people were powerful in the trade of the Moslem world and sometimes occupied important posts of State.

Meanwhile, in Christian Byzantium and Spain, the Jews were suspect as 'Asiatics' and were persecuted as potential allies of Islam. Relief came in Spain early in the eighth century with the Moslem conquest, and by the eleventh century that land was a great centre of Jewish culture. Then, as dynastic feuds weakened the Moslem hold, the Christian power gathering in northern Spain began to court the Jews; and, in the new Christian kingdom of Castile, Alphonso VI allowed them to enter the twelfth century under magnanimous tolerance. In Italy, rather remote from the Moslem menace, the Popes from Gregory I to Gregory VI encouraged the Jews to settle, and in Rome itself there was a large Jewish settlement whose members felt sufficient confidence to engage in public religious disputation. Similarly in France, the Jews settled in Paris and Orleans and elsewhere; and, after Charlemagne was crowned in A.D. 800 as Holy Roman Emperor, they spread into Germany and Central Europe too. Scattered now over most of the civilized world, keeping to a strict code of morality both in private life and in business, the Jews became the natural mediators between the Christian west and the Moslem east.

In A.D. 1096 however, the First Crusade marked the mounting of Christendom's offensive against Islam, and the Jews soon came in for persecution with other 'infidels'. In A.D. 1215 the Fourth Lateran Council revived for Jew and Moslem the yellow patch earlier imposed on Christian and Jew. And, as the Christian merchant and artisan class gained strength, the Jews were increasingly excluded from their former occupations and forced into peddling and the second-hand trade and the ungrateful role of moneylender. At the end of the thirteenth century they were expelled from England, in the fourteenth century from France, and in the fifteenth century the Spanish persecution reached its climax and destroyed the centre of Jewish civilization. Only in Italy, where the Jews had access to the Papal throne and (at a price) could gain protection, did some sort of tolerance continue. During this period of Christian persecution, the refugee stream flowed from west to east, into Poland and Russia and the Turkish Empire.

Following the Reformation, Luther found like Mohammed before him that the Jews were not to be won for his faith, and they learned to expect no sympathy from the Reformed Church. Fortunately, German Jewry gained letters of protection in the middle of the sixteenth century from the Emperor Charles V, and soon some of its members were important at the imperial court. In Poland too, Jewry thrived for a while, but eventually the ghetto was established throughout the Catholic world. In the seventeenth century hundreds of Jewish communities were destroyed in Poland and Russia, and now the stream of refugees flowed west and into Protestant Holland and England. Again a Jewish class of capitalists thrived in Europe, and in the eighteenth century

Jewry found new freedom through the American Independence and the French Revolution. In the early nineteenth century, over most of the civilized world, the problem was in the main no longer public persecution, or even legal discrimination, but a more subtle personal anti-Semitism.

In the latter half of the nineteenth century, unfortunately, the situation was sharpened both by increasing nationalism and by a developing ideology of race. To the religious intolerance of Jews as the people who had rejected Jesus, to suspicion of them as a group with many international connexions, to envy of their success in many branches of commerce, there was added the pseudo-scientific concept of the Jews as a so-called 'race'. The precise nature of anti-Semitism varied in its structure from one land to another, but usually it included these four elements. In England, it was possible for Disraeli, a Christian of Jewish ancestry, to become Prime Minister; but Jews could not join the 'best' clubs. In France, it was possible for Dreyfus to make a military career; but it was also possible for anti-Semites to secure his false condemnation. The Czarist régime in Russia used the Jewish people as the scapegoats of its tyranny and oppression; and eventually, following 1932, the German Nazis raised this persecution to its mad and evil climax.

This brief summary of the varied fortunes of Jewry, largely concentrated today in the U.S.A. and the U.S.S.R. and now at last established again in Israel, is sufficient to indicate that Jewish history, like the histories of other peoples, is a long and complex story with its glories and its degradations. And, while only the specialist can be expected to know its details, every teacher of history might at least equip himself with an adequate knowledge of the history of the Jewish settlement in his own country. Naturally, historical facts will not suffice to extirpate anti-Semitism, which is a plant most resistant to uprooting. First the teacher, and then the pupil, will have to go slowly through the sometimes painful process of purging himself of prejudice, and quick results will not easily be come by. Similarly, in a generation which has witnessed a rising tide of colour tension and which has seen the white man's pride of paleness matched by mounting anti-White militance, we cannot expect an easy solution to the problems of pigment-consciousness. Having so often suffered unfairly, the member of a minority group is liable to imagine injustice even where it does not exist, and the most tolerant majority-member may meet deeply wounding rebuffs. The dragon's teeth of racial discrimination are sprouting, and the resulting crop of calamity will be a heavy one. Anything which the teacher can do to strengthen his pupils' power of resistance to the disease of racialism will be an invaluable service to mankind.

10. The Idea of Racial Inequality

Although today few will be found to justify the grosser forms of racial discrimination and exploitation, there is still a fairly widespread feeling that 'coloured' people are in some way inferior to 'white' people. And such is the power of the preconceptions of the predominant group that many 'coloured' people themselves share this idea of their inferiority. It is a feeling rather than a belief, vague and ill-defined rather than clear-cut and definite, based on prejudice rather than on reason. There is, in fact, as we have already said, no very useful sense in which it may legitimately be said that one ethnic group is inherently superior to another.

The teacher knows, better than most people, that deep-seated prejudice cannot be quickly removed merely by factual evidence and logical argument; but this does not mean that facts and arguments are powerless. On the contrary, the very reason why the racial bigot so often seeks to buttress his belief by non-facts, which he believes or pretends to be facts, is that in even the most prejudiced of us there is some inner need for logical justification. If one 'fact' is proved false, the bigot will fall back on another, and then on another, and then on another; but, when at last the time comes that a prejudice is left without any protective façade of 'fact' at all, some basic re-thinking may take place. It is, therefore, worth the teacher's while to consider with his pupils in some detail this matter of 'racial superiority' and to demonstrate its essential fallaciousness. Superiority is a measure of value, and without a specified scale of values the word 'superior' is without meaning.

'What', the teacher may ask, 'is meant by the statement that People A is superior to People B?', and with his class he may build up a list of possible meanings. The list will begin something like this:

1. People A has a higher cultural level than People B.
2. People A is in physical character further removed from our pre-human ancestors than People B.
3. People A is endowed with a more efficiently functioning body than People B.
4. People A is innately more intelligent than People B.
5. People A is innately more moral or more temperamentally balanced than is People B.

And so the list might continue. Once a pupil has seen how complex is the original apparently simple statement, he may already begin to have some doubts on the matter. And, as each of the possible meanings of the statement is considered, critically and calmly and dispassionately, with the relevant evidence presented to the pupils—but not forced down perhaps unwilling throats—eventually the sheer prejudice will have to be faced in its shameful nakedness. Some pupils, perhaps, will still cling to their prejudice even when it has been stripped of its tattered clothing; but, in other cases, they may come to feel that the prejudice is an incubus, and will cast its weight away with feelings of relief.

The first criterion, that of cultural level, is one repeatedly met with in school lessons, and the teacher has many opportunities to clarify the muddied waters of popular belief. It is true that, during recent centuries, the 'pink' peoples have in general reached a higher level of civilization (certainly of technological achievements) than the browns and yellows and blacks, but history shows that it has not always been so. The English child, learning about the invasion of his land by the legions of Julius Caesar, is usually told that his forebears were stained with woad and roughly clad in animal pelts, but he may be surprised to learn that Cicero advised Atticus not to buy British slaves since 'they are so utterly stupid and incapable of learning'. European children, and those of European descent, might learn that during earlier centuries, when the lands that are now Germany and France and Scandinavia were backward and ignorant, there was a brilliant flowering of Hellenistic culture in the North African city of Alexandria and that in the Arab States the lamp of learning burned brightly. In the 'Middle Ages', Marco Polo travelled the territories of Tartary and chronicled the wonders that met his eye, and West Africa had its Ghana kingdom so admired by Arab voyagers. Before the fifteenth century, the African State of Benin was producing its little masterpieces of bronze and ivory; in the sixteenth, one of the great centres of Moslem culture was the University of Timbuktu; in the seventeenth, across the globe in China, there was the exquisite civilization of the early Manchu dynasty.

Cultural achievement at any one moment in history is no evidence of innate superiority, but depends upon all sorts of economic, social, political and geographical conditions. The idea that only the 'white' peoples are capable of high culture cannot withstand for a moment the ineluctable facts of history: the teacher who presents the facts to his pupils need scarcely draw the moral, for it is manifest. Moreover, it is quite unjustifiable to assess the level of a culture by reference solely to its technical achievements. Who is to say that the invention of electrical appliances, or the making of machines, or proficiency in plumbing, is 'superior' to philosophical insight, or to a rich and stable family life, or to generous hospitality?

Unfortunately, the textbooks used in schools do not commonly consider questions of this sort: more often, they tell whatever redounds to the credit of the country in which they are written. No objective teaching of history can exclude consideration of the enslavement of Africans and the exploitation of Asians by the powers of Europe; nor, if it is to avoid one-sidedness, can it fail to indicate that in earlier days Africans enslaved each other, and Asians exploited Asians. But this is no reason for failing to disclose the darker side of European dominance. The good teacher will not allow himself to be circumscribed by narrowly national books, and there are publications available[1] which will help him to teach history more impartially.

Geography books, too, may be misleading. Not uncommonly they imply, and in some cases explicitly state, that one so-called 'race' is superior to another. Especially is this the case with textbooks used in the schools of a colonial power, where the natives of an African colony may be described as 'child-like' and as having been 'uncivilized until the more energetic and intelligent white man came'. In European schools, there is a tendency for textbooks to imply the inferiority of the Amerindians and Australoids whom the Europeans decimated, of the Negroids whom they once enslaved, and of the Asiatics whom they in the past exploited. Similarly, some of the textbooks commonly used in United States schools give inadequate information on ethnic matters and do little to promote racial tolerance. They sometimes present a picture of 'the American way of life' which implies that it is 'white', Protestant and middle-class, and which omits all reference to segregation and discrimination. They often imply that Negroes as a group are child-like and contented, and other ethnic groups may similarly be represented by unreal stereotypes. The Amerindian is often described in the framework of frontier days, appearing either as a noble savage or as a cold-blooded scalper, and reference is rarely made to the position of Indians in modern American life. Negroes, Jews, those whose origins were in Mexico or China or Japan—these important groups of American citizens are often ignored in descriptions of American society, and as a result the impression may be given (perhaps quite unintentionally) that they are somehow less American than the majority group. The

1. See *History Textbooks and International Understanding,* by J. A. Lauwerys, published by Unesco (Paris, 1953). A brief survey of history books commonly used in English schools is given in *History Without Bias?,* by E. H. Dance (Council of Christians and Jews, London, 1954).

teacher owes it to his pupils to correct the errors and make good the deficiencies of any books which offend in these ways, exactly as he would if his chemistry or mathematics textbooks were similarly deficient.[1]

In schools which have complete freedom of choice of the books they will use, it may be possible to choose texts which are less objectionable on this score. In schools for which the books are prescribed by some central educational agency, teachers' suggestions for improvement may lead to the omission of offending matter and the insertion of desirable material in future editions. But, in any case, implications of inherent ethnic superiority-inferiority should not be allowed to go unchallenged.

Nor is it only the text that may mislead in this way: the camera can lie very effectively if its lens is suitably pointed. Thus, if the only photographs of 'Blacks' in a geography book show them with mud-matted hair and skewers through their noses, while the photographs of 'Whites' depict them in elegant linen and fine footwear, an impression of Negro inferiority is almost inevitably given. And, as schools increasingly use films and other visual aids of various kinds, it will become the more essential that teachers examine all such materials with a critical eye. Meanwhile, the commercial cinema misleads many a child: on the screen, Negroes tend to appear either as bloodthirsty warriors or as lovable children, Orientals either as sinister plotters or as sleek sophisticates, and non-Europeans generally as menial servants. All too often, unfortunately, teachers tend to turn up their noses at the local cinema and thereby abandon their pupils to its distorting influence. If teachers would make a habit of discussing with their children the 'film of the week', they would find many an opportunity of correcting false impressions. No one ever knows in advance exactly where such discussions with secondary school pupils will lead; but, so long as they tread territory which is real and not imaginary, the precise details

1. See *A Handbook of Suggestions on the Teaching of Geography* (*Towards World Understanding*—X), published by Unesco (Paris, 1951).

of the route do not greatly matter. On one occasion it may be discovered that the Arab peoples developed an effective way of manipulating numbers, and that 'algebra' is an Arab word; on another occasion attention might be drawn to the metallurgical skill of the early peoples of India; on another occasion there may be mentioned the Chinese invention of paper, porcelain, gunpowder, printing and the magnetic compass—without, of course, implying that such inventions were the result of innate superiority, any more than were the more numerous inventions of Europeans. It is not by a single set lesson that the teacher can eradicate prejudices deeply rooted, but only by the infinitely patient reiteration and exemplification of truth wherever and whenever opportunity offers. There are now available admirable documentary films giving accurate and balanced pictures of the achievements and ways of life of many peoples, and the wise teacher will make effective use of them. In some countries, radio and television programmes may also be useful in correcting misconceptions about 'race': elsewhere, unfortunately, such programmes powerfully perpetuate offensive stereotypes.

Sometimes—as a rule unintentionally—teachers themselves are responsible for confirming their pupils' ideas of ethnic inferiority. In a praiseworthy effort to inject interest and romance into their history and geography lessons, teachers may concentrate unduly on the ways in which other peoples *differ* from their own. Thus, children will learn about African drumming and Ashanti warriors, about Chinese mandarins and water-buffaloes in rice-fields, about 'Red Indian' Chiefs and the scalping of the early American settlers. It would be better if such lessons were to deal more often with the way in which children in West Africa go to school and university, the way in which the citizens of China conduct large-scale businesses and build great factories, the way in which some Amerindians do all the things which other Americans do. Some English schools have established regular postal communication with schools in Nigeria and elsewhere, and the letters received and read in class do a good deal to disabuse the pupils of false notions about the daily lives of their correspondents. Once the child is convinced that those of different ethnic origin are similar to himself in fundamentals, he can delight in strange and often picturesque distinctions: before he has the assurance of such a basic conviction, lessons about the distinctions may serve only to prevent an appreciation of the fundamental similarity.

As to the second possible criterion of 'superiority', that of the evolutionary differentiation of physical characters, the position of the three major ethnic groups is roughly as follows. In hairiness of body the Caucasoids are clearly the most primitive (i.e. the most similar to our ape-like ancestors) of the three groups, while the Negroids, with their smooth almost hairless skins, are clearly the most advanced (i.e. the most different from our ape-like ancestors). In skin colour it is impossible to say whether 'white', 'yellow' or 'black' is the most advanced, since we do not know with any certainty what our ancestors' skin colour was. But most hairy apes and monkeys have whitish skin, and it may be that the Negroids developed dark skin as an alternative form of protection from the sun when they lost their body hair. In general facial conformation, and in the possession of a broad nose, the Negroid is nearer to the primitive pattern; while, in having thin compressed lips and rather straight lank hair, the Caucasoid is the nearer. It would therefore be difficult to strike a balance between the different degrees of primitiveness of this character and that; but, if a balance were struck, it is doubtful whether the 'Whites' would be accounted the most advanced in evolution of the three great ethnic divisions of mankind.

As regards the third possible criterion of superiority, that of efficiency of bodily functioning, the position seems to be roughly what we would expect. On the whole, the Negroid body (with its darker skin, wider nose and more numerous sweat glands) functions rather better in hot equatorial conditions, and the Caucasoid body (with its lighter skin, narrower nose and fewer sweat glands) functions rather better in cool temperate conditions. But, in any event, the differences are slight. Moreover, the teacher will wish his pupils to recognize that the biological significance of hereditary differences depends upon the environmental conditions. In the absence of the amenities of civilization, the Englishman would be the more likely to suffer from skin diseases in sunny Nigeria and the Nigerian more likely to suffer from vitamin D deficiency in cloudy England; but, since the Englishman in Nigeria can use protective clothes or skin-creams and the Nigerian in England can take cod-liver oil, their differences in skin colour are of no great importance. With each advance in scientific knowledge and technical invention, our cultural environment becomes increasingly important and our hereditary peculiarities less restrictive. Biological differences in this character or that, which in early ages may have made Europeans 'superior' in Europe and 'inferior' in Africa, or Africans 'superior' in Africa and 'inferior' in Europe, are not today of great significance.

Usually, however, when people speak of 'racial' superiority or inferiority, they are thinking of intellectual or moral and temperamental factors; and the thinking is often very muddled. Some writers quote figures showing that on the average Europeans have larger brains than Africans, and imply that the European is therefore on the average more intelligent than the Negro. If this argument were valid, we should have to admit that certain African Kaffir groups, with brains larger than Europeans, were yet more intelligent; while certain Ice Age men, who had exceptionally large brains, must have been intellectual giants. In fact, however, there is no such simple relation between brain size and intelligence, so all these measurements are entirely irrelevant. If we want to compare the intelligence of different population groups, we must measure their intellectual processes, not their cranial capacities.

Teachers should be more aware than most people that we have no way of measuring innate intellectual ability as such, even if such a thing exists. True, if we have a group of children brought up from birth in the one community and in fairly similar homes, we can by means of standardized tests grade the children not too inaccurately in respect of intelligence; but even in these circumstances the results are confused by all sorts of environmental factors. When we come to the enormously more complex problem of different ethnic groups, talking different tongues and dwelling in different lands, living different lives and from birth building up different ways of thought, we have to admit that intelligence tests are very shaky instruments indeed. There is little doubt that most of the so-called 'differences in racial intelligence' which have sometimes been reported are the result of variations in physical or cultural environment rather than of variations in heredity.[1] For example, although Negro recruits to the U.S. Army from the Southern states, where their educational and other opportunities are restricted, scored lower than did the Whites, Negroes from some of the Northern states (where there is comparatively little such restriction) scored higher than did the Whites from some of the Southern states. Similarly, Amerindian children of the Osage tribe, who have been fortunate enough to profit from oil wells on their reservation and so have good schools and general living conditions, score at least as highly as the white children at similar schools.

Thus, to summarize, we may say that we have no means of measuring hereditary intellectual and temperamental capacity free of environmental influence, that measurements which purport to show differences in average intelligence between different ethnic groups living in different cultures are worthless, that observations on members of different groups living under similar conditions tend to show that there are no significant ethnic differences in intelligence, and that in any event the range of intelligence within any one ethnic group is very much greater than has even been suggested as a difference between the average intelligence of different groups. Or, more briefly, that while it is not inconceivable that the so-called 'races' might differ in intellectual capacity, there is little or no evidence to indicate that they do so differ. Similarly, as anyone can see in communities the world over, peoples of many ethnic origins demonstrate a wide range of emotional

1. For further details of the intellectual ability of different ethnic groups, see Otto Klineberg's booklet *Race and Psychology*, published by Unesco (Paris, 1951).

and temperamental qualities which enable them to be useful members of societies of all sorts.

However, even if at some future time it were shown that there were in fact some ethnic differences of an intellectual or temperamental nature, this would not necessarily imply superiority or inferiority. People may differ in all sorts of ways, but difference is one thing and superiority is another. Red hair is different from black hair, but is neither superior nor inferior to it—the two are different, but of equal status. The same could apply to some mental differences. Moreover, the teacher whose daily life is spent with children of very different physiques, intellectual abilities and temperamental characteristics, and who yet tries to treat them all as individual human beings with equal rights to his care and consideration, will need no convincing that the condemnation of racial discrimination does not depend upon any proof that all ethnic groups have identical physical or mental or emotional endowments. Even if all 'white' children were stronger than all 'black' children or if all 'black' children were cleverer than all 'white' children, the teacher would still regard it as his duty to do his utmost to foster the development of each individual. And, in the same way, the teacher will wish to do all he can to encourage attitudes of racial toleration in his pupils, quite irrespective of any proof that different ethnic groups are equal in this or that ability. Nevertheless, if he can show how baseless—indeed, how nearly meaningless—this idea of 'racial superiority' is, he will find it easier to combat what prejudices may be present in his pupils.

There does remain, of course, one sense in which it might be proper to say 'People A is superior to People B'. It might be, for example, that 60 per cent of People A reached a certain intelligence level and that only 50 per cent of People B reached that same level under equal conditions; or it might be that 80 per cent of People A and only 70 per cent of People B were capable of a certain physical skill. But, even if this were proved to be the case, it would still remain nonsensical to label the individual with the statistical average ability of his group rather than with his own individual ability.

Very often, the warmly hero-worshipping mind of adolescence will be less vividly impressed by sustained and reasoned argument than by striking individual examples of physical, intellectual, temperamental and moral greatness in people of different ethnic origins; and there will be many opportunities in the school to mention examples of outstanding achievement by members of various ethnic and so-called 'racial' groups.

Yet not too much should be made of this 'eminent individuals' approach to the matter. In the first place it is a simple fact that thus far in history there have been comparatively few Negroes of the highest culture, and many of them have been of mixed Negroid-Caucasoid ancestry. Second, and more important, to overstress that there are great Negroes and Asians and Jews may seem to imply that racial tolerance should be dependent on such greatness, which is going a long way to grant one of the very premises of racial bigotry. It may, moreover, make some children of minority groups feel that they must win acceptance in the school by distinguishing themselves in some way, and thus produce either excessive strain or objectionable aggressiveness. In the case of the Jewish people in particular, their history is so studded with human greatness that there may be danger in stressing what is, for some Gentiles, already an unconscious source of envy and resentment. If, however, there is evidence in the classroom of damaging ignorance on this point, the teacher should certainly quote one or two cases to illustrate Jewish ability.

It has been remarked that 'every people has a right to have its scoundrels', and this puts the question in its proper perspective. When a Jewish financier cheats his shareholders or a Negro soldier rapes a girl, the words 'Jewish' and 'Negro' are likely to figure prominently in newspaper headlines; when the offenders are Gentile or White, their ethnic affiliations are usually not mentioned. This circular process of labelling the group with the offences of a few delinquent members, and then labelling the members of the group with the attached delinquencies, is responsible for the maintenance of much group prejudice; and it is no more honest to seek to parallel the process with the achievements of a few persons of distinction. The important thing is for our pupils to learn to judge each individual *as an individual,* neither owning the glory nor bearing the shame of other individuals in his group; and that is a matter for long and persistent effort on the teacher's part. And, most essential, the whole day-by-day conduct of the school should be directed towards building up better ways of thinking and feeling in general, so that the pupils learn to think straight and feel charitably when confronted with any individual or group different from themselves.

11. The Emotive Power of Words

No one who has ever felt the contempt which is sometimes put into the word 'nigger' or 'yid' or 'wop' or 'greaser' can have much doubt about the emotional content of such terms. True, when the English child learns the nursery rhyme about the 'Ten Little Nigger Boys' who sat down to dine, the word 'nigger' is used in a warm, friendly way; but words have an emotive power for the listener as well as for the speaker, and many Negroes rise in resentment at what they imagine to be racial prejudice. Similarly, although the word 'Negress' may be used in its simple descriptive sense, without any offensive intent, it may nevertheless carry objectionable connotations of the days when plantation owners took female slaves as concubines, and may even in part offend because it unconsciously recalls the animal names 'lioness' and 'tigress'. Or, to take another example, the words 'Jew' and 'Jewess' are in essence simply classificatory terms, no more objectionable than 'author' and 'authoress'; yet, so sensitive to possibilities of anti-Semitic prejudice have some individuals become, they will circumlocute about 'a man (or a woman) of the Hebrew faith' to avoid the risk of giving offence. Just as, in poetry, certain words have not only a surface significance but also a rich emotional content which gives them layer upon layer of meaning, so many words relating to race have complex associations which insinuate subtle intimations of prejudice. And, if the child is to learn to use his native language really well, he must become aware of this complex quality of words.

Take the adjectives 'black', 'brown', 'yellow' and 'white'. Applied to paints or fabrics, they are simply descriptive words implying nothing beyond the facts of colour difference. But use them in the phrases 'black race', 'brown race', 'yellow race' and 'white race'—and how subtly the adjectives imply grades of merit and demerit! Usually unrecognized on the conscious level, but often a potent catalyst of emotion, 'white' now becomes set apart from the other three colour adjectives, and carries with it an idea of basic cleanliness which 'black' and 'brown' and 'yellow' do not share. Then white is the symbol of purity and virginity, while black has all the unsavoury associations of blackmail and blackleg and blackguard. There is also white as 'not-coloured', while black and brown and yellow are 'coloured'—an implication which becomes explicit when 'coloured' is used as a synonym or euphemism for 'Negro'. The white man's pride of colour is understandable as a reflection of his several centuries' technical superiority, but it has become associated in many minds with the idea that 'whiteness' itself is in some way superior to brownness or yellowness or blackness. This complex emotional content of the word 'white' would become apparent to children of European origin if, for a period, they and their teacher deliberately used the rather more accurate epithet 'pink' in classroom discussion of ethnic differences. The sense of superiority which comes to many people when they think of themselves as being white rather than yellow or brown is liable to diminish when they think of themselves as pink, and the thrill of horror which is aroused in some by the idea of intermarriage between black and white may be somewhat less acute at the thought of the mingling of black and pink.

This word 'mingling', too, is richly emotive in the context of race. 'Mingling', or 'mixture', is often expressive of adulteration or impurity: there is the dishonest dairyman mixing water with his milk, there is the appalling consequence of sewage becoming mingled with drinking water. As for the phrase 'mixed blood', it carries not only the emotive implications of 'mixed ' but also the extremely powerful surcharging of the word 'blood': it is not surprising that many people, who regard a 'pure' African or a 'pure' European or a 'pure' Indian with equal respect, view a person of 'mixed blood' with something approaching loathing. One speaks of one's child as being 'of my own blood'; there is the common saying 'blood is thicker than water'; the closest ties of comradeship are those between 'blood brothers'; there are the metaphors of 'blue blood', 'plebeian blood' and 'new blood'; orators may arouse high passion by talk of 'British blood' or 'Russian blood' or 'American blood'; bigots may even speak of 'yellow blood' and 'white blood' and 'black blood'. Blood is the very life-stream and its mythology is rich and varied. But the word 'blood' should never be used as if it meant 'inherited constitution'.

Quite apart from any emotively powerful socio-historical connotations, there are some words whose very semantic structure seems to assert a kind of derogation. For example, the words 'half-caste'—with its implication on the one hand of something less-than-complete and on the other hand of something to be ranked in a scale of social value—and 'mulatto'—in its first syllable faintly reminiscent of the hybrid progeny of the horse and ass, and in its ending evoking memories of the sinister stiletto—have a colouring whose effect on sentiment may be far more complex than is usually recognized. And, while it is primarily for the biology teacher to provide children with factual knowledge about genes, it is the task of the teacher of language to sharpen his pupils' awareness of the ways in which words may carry complex intimations of meaning. To recognize the existence of irrational feelings is often the first step towards liberating oneself from them, and the teacher can contribute a good deal to the emotional emancipation of his pupils by helping them to understand how it is that certain words and phrases come to arouse feelings of this kind.

Since the great writers are great precisely because they

know how to handle words effectively, it is not surprising that children may be deeply influenced in their attitudes by the literature which they read in school. Thus, if Shakespeare's play *Othello* is badly taught, it may arouse feelings of fear and even horror of the powerful Moor; but, taught well, revealing all its power of characterization, it tends rather to increase the pupils' sensitivity to the vast range of human vice and virtue. Similarly with *The Merchant of Venice*: it can be so produced as to present Shylock simply as a snivelling creature typical of the base Jewish people—or, on the other hand, its production can focus attention on the way in which a Jew may be made to suffer by a harsh Gentile world. Properly interpreted, this play—like all great tragedies—should above all sensitize its auditors to the qualities of excellence and baseness and to the complexity of the human situation.

Some teachers, in a creditable determination to do nothing to perpetuate false racial stereotypes, refrain from reading with their children any books in which a member of a minority group appears in discreditable light. But literature is a mirror held up to life and, if the image is at all distorted, it is more profitable to examine the reasons for the distortion than to try to hide the mirror. Shakespeare is not a soporific; he richly reflects human nature in all its infinite variety and catalyses consideration of the vagaries of human action. Let pupils read some passages from Marlowe's *Jew of Malta,* let them learn that in the days when Shakespeare and Marlowe were writing a Jew had been falsely accused of a plot against Queen Elizabeth, and they will understand why anti-Semitism enters the drama. So with Dickens's picture of the nineteenth-century English underworld: good and bad appear, Gentile and Jew alike, and only the already prejudiced could pretend that it is the Jew as such who shows up badly. Fagin is not the only, or even the worst, villain in *Oliver Twist,* and we can always set against him the favourable picture of a Jew in Eliot's *Daniel Deronda.* The banning of books is no way to deal with false stereotypes: one might as well ban a child from bathing instead of teaching him how to swim.

Stereotypes do not, without some reason, come into existence and spread widely and retain a stubborn hold on many minds. Merely to condemn a stereotype—or, *a fortiori,* to condemn the child who holds it—achieves nothing except a warm glow of self-satisfied rectitude in the person who makes the condemnation, and perhaps a damaging sense of guilt in the child rebuked. The important thing is to understand the origins of stereotypes and the precise natures of their falseness and the ways in which minds can be liberated from them. Complete intellectual honesty is essential, and with it an all-embracing charity of spirit. And the fact is that some stereotypes have become established, or at least have been given a superficial air of verisimilitude, because at some time there has been some element of truth in them. Uncle Tom in his cabin is today a stereotype utterly remote from the reality and even more from the potentiality of the Negro people; yet under the conditions in which he lived there were in fact many Negroes like him. Huckleberry Finn's Negro neighbour Jim showed a subservience in no way innate in Negro nature; but thousands of Jims were conditioned to such subservience by the society which oppressed them. When colonial territories contained 'lesser breeds without the law', many members of those breeds survived by stealth and slyness and dishonesty; when Jews were refused full civic status and were hounded from land to land, many turned their backs on their neighbours and concentrated on their international connexions. Since all peoples are infinitely varied, no stereotype is ever true; but, since all peoples receive the impress of their social state, many stereotypes have, or at some past time have had, just that trace of truth necessary to render them credible to the credulous. What the teacher can do is help his pupils to identify these feeble foundations of fact, recognize the specific conditions which may have given them some slight semblance of reality, isolate them from the fantastic framework of fallacy which has been erected on them, and show how the whole building collapses under the impact of intelligent inspection.

Some American schools have had a good deal of experience in using literature as a means of enriching their pupils' human relations in general and racial attitudes in particular.[1] Fiction, biography and drama may be potent means of sensitizing young people to the varieties of human character and experience, thus making it easier for them to enter sympathetically into the experience of those of different ethnic and cultural groups. Good literature, too, can encourage an awareness of the infinite complexity of human good and evil, so fostering a suspicion of oversimplified judgements of other peoples' actions.

It may well be that a book, which could be of the greatest significance in the emotional and social maturation of one child in a class, would utterly fail to catch the interest of another or convey any significance to him. If the reader is to identify himself emotionally with the characters portrayed, or even to make emotional contact with them, he must himself have had, or at least have imaginatively conceived, experiences not too remote from theirs. Some great books are of a genius so universal that all succeeding generations of schoolchildren can enter into them, but in addition the teacher may recommend reading to individual children on the basis of their individual needs and abilities: naturally, this implies that the teacher will both read a book before recommending it and study the child before setting him a book to read.

Du Bose Heyward's *Mamba's Daughter*[2] and William Manner's *Father and the Angels*[3] can respectively illuminate the patterns of life of a Southern Negro family and the family of a Jewish rabbi; while Carl Glick's *Shake Hands with the Dragon*[4] tells of the daily life of New Yorkers of Chinese origin, and Sholem Asch's *East River*[5] describes the richly teeming life of a polyethnic immigrant community. In his

---

1. See especially *Literature for Human Understanding* and *Reading Ladders for Human Relations,* both by Hilda Taba *et al.* (American Council on Education, Washington, D.C., 1948 and 1949). The latter gives synopses of many novels and biographies, with indications of the types of children for whom they may be suitable.
2. Published by Doubleday (New York, 1929).
3. Published by Dutton (New York, 1947).
4. Published by McGraw (New York, 1941).
5. Published by Putnam (New York, 1946).

The Pearl[1] John Steinbeck paints a bitter yet beautiful picture of the poverty-stricken fishermen of Mexico; the beauty and the tragic dilemma of South Africa are exquisitely shown in Alan Paton's *Cry the Beloved Country,*[2] while Howard Fast's *Freedom Road*[3] poignantly portrays the fate of the freed slaves of South Carolina in Reconstruction days. Such books, read with wise guidance, can do much to extend the understanding and increase the sensitivity of older children in their dealings with people different from themselves.

When a book is read by a group of children or by the class as a whole, the reading may profitably be followed by questioning and discussion. An exchange of views on the problems posed by the story may help the class to come to a common conclusion on their proper solution; and, even if no agreement is reached, something will have been gained by the unreserved ventilation and honest consideration of conflicting opinions. Sometimes incidents may be dramatized, so that the pupils enter more fully into the feelings of the characters they play: a child of the majority group who acts the part of a member of a despised minority, and is subjected even if only in surrogate to humiliation and exclusion, may become more vividly aware of the deeply wounding pricks of group prejudice.

Group sentiment is a complex thing, deriving in part from awareness of kinship, in part from common locality, from a shared history or a shared religion, or from a community of economic interest. And, so powerful is group sentiment liable to grow, the great moral leaders of mankind have frequently found it necessary to issue warnings against the discrimination in which it often results. 'The stranger that dwelleth with you shall be unto you as one born among you, and thou shalt love him as thyself', says the book of Leviticus, and the book of Numbers also told the Jews, 'One ordinance shall be both for you of the congregation, and also for the stranger that sojourneth with you.' Yet, without destroying

1. Published by Viking (New York, 1947).
2. Published by Cape (London, 1948).
3. Published by Pocket Books (New York, 1944).

that group sentiment, which is entirely proper and desirable, it is possible to do something to remove the obstacles to clear vision which is its common accompaniment.

The ingenious teacher of language will be able to find ways[1] to provide children with practice in the objective reporting of events, the critical comparison of varying accounts by different observers, the detection of errors and absurdities in statements and arguments, the honest examination of their own preconceptions and prejudices, and the discernment of motives in others and in themselves. Newspapers, periodicals and 'comic' illustrated magazines may be searched for misleading matter, school textbooks may be subjected to critical examination, local or topical discriminatory incidents discussed. In this manner, while avoiding the danger of mere verbal quibbling and destructive disparagement, it should be possible to encourage in children attitudes unfavourable to the growth of racial prejudice. And thus, building on the earlier and narrower loyalties to family and friends and community and nation, we may foster a feeling of belonging to humanity as a whole.

It is, however, not only in the language or literature lesson that opportunities arise to help children to cope with the complex emotional content of words. Such words may crop up in virtually any subject of the school curriculum, and it is therefore important that all teachers should be prepared to deal with them as they arise. The biology lesson, for example, may present a suitable occasion to isolate the proper meaning of 'pure-bred', as a genetically descriptive term, from the implications of virtue and superiority which often attach to it. The history or geography lesson may give the teacher a chance to distinguish the descriptive sense of 'hordes' and 'tribes' from their accompanying suggestions of crude violence and primitive ignorance. In almost any subject of the curriculum, the enormous emotive power of the word 'blood' may make itself felt, and care can be taken that this power

1. Some useful suggestions are made in the booklet *In the Classroom* (*Towards World Understanding*—V), published by Unesco (Paris, 1949).

does not, as it may very easily do, carry over into the pupils' attitudes to race relations.

So with the very word 'race' itself. Passing into general usage in its present sense after Buffon gave it the seal of his approval in 1749, the word had formerly been used in the wider sense of 'the human race', and in the narrower sense of the posterity of a person, as in the phrase 'the race of Abraham'. And, subtly still today, the word carries with it something of these earlier connotations, so that the members of another 'race' are not quite human—or not quite one's own kith and kin. And, as a result, many a man who is well aware of the scientific facts about race is nevertheless unable to cast off completely his irrational feelings about it. He is, indeed, in much the same position as was Madame de Staël, who is reported to have said, 'I do not believe in ghosts, but I am afraid of them.' We must help our pupils to pass beyond the stage of abandoning fallacious beliefs, and to progress into the stage of getting rid also of irrational fears.

12. The Tangled Roots of Prejudice

Racial prejudice has many roots,[1] and the teacher who would combat it needs to know how complex and confused these roots may be. Peoples' attitudes and sentiments and behaviour are not determined on a purely rational basis; facts do not 'speak for themselves'—they speak to each person differently, according to his prejudices and preconceptions. Thus the teacher has to do much more than merely tell his pupils the biological and sociological facts about race: he has to help to whittle away preconceptions held since infancy, to dissolve

1. The matter is well discussed by Arnold M. Rose in his booklet *The Roots of Prejudice*, published by Unesco (Paris, 1951).

irrational prejudices, and to erode false ideas sometimes held with almost wilful persistence. He may find that his pupils' attitudes have component feelings of envy and apprehension, distrust and fear, resentment and guilt, and sometimes deeply disguised sexual or destructive impulses. Only by getting to know his pupils well as individuals, and treating them as individuals, can he hope to dig down to these tangled roots of prejudice.

And how very tangled those roots may be! The same mother who has implanted in her daughter a horror of Negroes may also have provided her with the emotional security of her infant days; the very father who has brought up his son to despise the Jews may also have been the inspiration of his boyhood ambitions: it is not an easy thing, in such circumstances, to pull out poisonous prejudice without also dislodging essential loyalties. The process must be slow and patient, and carefully adjusted to each child's own individual needs. The teacher will be able to think of many ways of diagnosing these needs: the friendship of parents may be cultivated and the home background of the children discovered, the pupils may be persuaded to talk and write about their out-of-school activities and their likes and dislikes, classroom records of each member of the class may be kept and periodically consulted, simple 'word association' tests may be given to see how the children respond to words like 'Negro' and 'White' and 'Gentile' and 'Jew', and so on. But, whatever methods the teacher may choose to use, he must recognize that infinite patience will be needed.

It is sometimes supposed that young children are always free of racial prejudice, but this attractive picture of childhood innocence scarcely corresponds with the facts. From the very earliest days infants are imbibing the implicit assumptions of the society in which they live; and, if the social environment is one of racial discrimination, it will be difficult indeed for a child to grow up without taking it for granted that such a state of affairs is part of the natural order of things. If all the local physicians and lawyers are 'white', but many of the manual labourers 'black', he will tend to assume that those of darker skin are destined for the humbler roles of society.

If he overhears repeated adult references to the Jews as having this or that undesirable characteristic, he may well build up for himself a mental picture corresponding to such misrepresentations rather than to evident truth. If in his community any ethnic group mostly lives in slums, he is liable to think that the slum-fostered dirt and degradation is natural for that people. His parents' avoidance of social contact with those of different faith or colour, his neighbours' reluctance to allow children of another ethnic group into their houses, his playmates' rejection of children of different origin—all add up, as clearly as if the words were spoken, to the clear injunction 'Thou shalt be prejudiced'.

In some ways, racial prejudice and discrimination today play the same social role as did the persecution of the Christians and Jews in Imperial Rome, the crusades against the infidels in medieval Christendom, the inquisition of heretics and the burning of witches. All such attacks have these things usually in common—they provide a means of distracting the attention of the oppressed from the defects of their oppressors, they offer the opportunity of direct or indirect material gain, they serve to 'smear' a whole group of people indiscriminately and so aid charlatans and witch-hunters in their nefarious designs, and they provide a socially acceptable outlet for feelings of frustration and aggression. The early Christians of Rome were falsely accused of obscenity, ritual murder and disloyalty, and the group-prejudices of our own time are nourished by charges no less false. If Jews can be blamed both as the international capitalists and as the international communists—for intergroup prejudice knows no logic—the common people may be diverted from careful inquiry into the causes of the calamities which befall them. If Negroes can be stereotyped as stupid, a good excuse is provided for keeping them out of the skilled jobs desired by the 'white' workers. If all Europeans can be labelled as 'white devils', they can more easily be cast out from Asian lands. If the entire people of an African or Asian region can be characterized as 'terrorists', some sort of justification may be provided for denying them self-government and the protection of normal legal process. And, if the ordinary individual citizen of any land is feeling frustrated, racial myth provides a welcome sanction for the petty persecution of members of a scapegoat group.

There are divers factors in modern society which encourage feelings of frustration and aggression. We have a higher standard of living than our ancestors, but in many ways feel less secure. We know more about the physical nature of the world in which we live, but have less certainty about what life should be lived for. Society demands conformity in many matters, and in particular it places many restraints on sexual behaviour. Children—who are themselves a minority group in a peculiarly defenceless position—are from the earliest days prevented from doing this and that, and have to bottle up within themselves all sorts of impulses to activity. As a result, we may tend to project on to minority groups those urgent desires which we dare not acknowledge in ourselves —desires for domination, for violence, for a vigorous and unrestrained sex life, for wealth unbounded. And, having made the projection, we may hate the minority groups for what we have projected on to them.

Not only are fear and frustration potent sources of aggression, but the situation may be aggravated by feelings of inadequacy or guilt. One reason why anti-Semitism so flourished in Germany may have been that the German people, prevented by their late achievement of nationhood from establishing a world-wide empire like Britain's, found reassurance in the assertion of their 'Aryan' superiority. One reason why the Englishman, racially tolerant at home, so often develops racial prejudice in Africa and Asia, may be that there he represents a dominant minority group and fears the potential rebellion of the subservient native majority—a situation which today exists very clearly in South Africa. One reason why many 'Whites' from the Southern states of the U.S.A. are so virulent in their expression of racial prejudice is probably that, deep down, they feel guilty about the way in which the Negroes have been treated.

Wherever history or geography or civics lessons make it relevant to do so, the teacher can help to immunize his pupils against the development of intergroup prejudice by laying bare its basis in cases such as those mentioned above. Wherever erroneous stereotypes based on simple ignorance betray themselves in the child's comments, the teacher can supply the corrective in the form of further information. And, wherever such stereotypes are perpetuated by a pupil's refusal to recognize the facts, the teacher can gradually open his eyes for him and gently wash away the scales that cover them. There is, admittedly, no certainty that what the teacher does in the school to encourage an enlightened attitude to inter-group relations will have a permanent effect on pupils' behaviour once they leave school. But this is no reason for not performing the task that lies to hand: after all, it is a commonplace in education that we are uncertain what permanent effects this or that element in schooling may have, but we do not for that reason close down our schools. And in any event, controlled experiment has shown that it is in fact possible to change children's racial attitudes quite considerably by means of carefully devised educational procedures in the school.[1]

The teacher will often find that his pupils' prejudices have complex origins which are difficult to trace. For two or three centuries the Western world has been washed by the waves of racial and religio-racial discrimination, and its waters have seeped into the very fabric of our social thought. Thus, it will often be the faint whisper of prejudice, rather than its strident clamour, which the teacher with a sensitive ear will detect, and it is a whisper not easily stilled. The blatant lie can be exposed as plainly false and the crude political discrimination denounced as manifestly unjust, but the delicate denial of human fraternity which takes the form of not-quite-friendship is too subtle a thing to be conjured away easily. Only by patiently correcting month by month each minor manifestation of prejudice, and by demonstrating year by year a genuinely all-embracing acceptance of humanity, can the teacher hope finally to free his pupils of this more tenuous type of discrimination.

It is important that the teacher should provoke genuine discussion—not formal debate, which often tends to confirm

---

1. See *They Learn What They Live,* by Helen G. Trager and Marion R. Yarrow (Harper, New York, 1950).

speakers in their views and makes their abandonment a matter of loss of prestige—encouraging the pupils to express all points of view quite openly and freely. Any too obvious or premature disapproval of undesirable opinions may lead to their repression, but will not secure their eradication; and it is a poor service to ethnic understanding merely to suppress views, leaving them still potent and liable to break out with renewed virulence after the child has left school. Moreover, it must be remembered that the child who exhibits prejudice is as much in need of help as the child who is subjected to it, should be treated by the teacher with the same sympathy and understanding, and in some cases may actually need protection by the teacher from the indignation of classmates who resent all racial prejudice. The securer a child feels, the less emotional need he will have to indulge in discrimination: and the teacher must therefore take care, while indicating unambiguously his own tolerance, not to appear to reject the prejudiced pupil. Each child's self-respect must be built up in every possible way, and this can only be done if the teacher tries to enter into the mind of his pupil, no matter how much he may disapprove of its distortions and confusions and contradictions. It is a painful process, as any honest teacher will recognize from his own experience, to give up prejudices behind which one has sheltered for years, and we must not be surprised if our pupils offer unconscious resistance to efforts at their enlightenment. Any sudden and ruthless stripping away of a child's protective covering may in the long run do more harm than good; and the teacher should seek to be not a bulldozer, to demolish his pupils' illogicalities by brute force of argument, but rather a lightning conductor by which their emotional tensions and their accompanying prejudices may safely leak away.

Feelings of ethnic exclusiveness are not invariably due to a sense of superiority, for children often tend to withdraw from that which is merely different. In such cases it may be helpful to ask them to imagine a meeting between children of different colours in complete darkness: the sudden realization that in this event they could not tell a European from an African or Asian may be very salutary. Yet the child is often inclined to regard the unusual as the undesirable; and in some countries, where there are few folk of darker hue than pink and little active racial antagonism, there may be the feeling that darker-skinned people, being the exception, are in some way inferior. This does not always lead to distaste—it may, on the contrary, evoke an attitude of sympathy which nevertheless implies a sense of superiority—but it is a feeling based on falsehood, and the child should be freed from it. And this liberation may sometimes be achieved by the simple expedient of impressing on pupils, as geography lessons give innumerable opportunities to do, the simple fact that over three-fifths of the world's population are 'coloured' and that it is the 'Whites' who constitute a minority of unusual colour and physique.

Even more important, however, is the encouragement of appreciation of diversity in general. There is in the modern world altogether too widespread a tendency to uniformity and conformity in all things, and we are in danger of losing sight of the enormous human potentiality for idiosyncrasy and originality. We do not know what combinations of desirable characteristics, what possibilities of cultural diversity, may not await us in a world which ceases to measure all men by the yardstick of 'white' ways but which, instead, encourages peoples of all pigmentations to develop to the fullest their own innate qualities and to combine in the formation of fresh mixtures. Teachers, therefore, should not seek to minimize ethnic differences or to pretend that they do not exist, but rather to emphasize the uniqueness of each individual human person and to encourage children to appreciate the value of human variation.

One element in racial prejudice is sometimes of an aesthetic nature: the child brought up to admire Greek statues and the paintings of the Italian Renaissance is often conditioned against skins that are not white and locks that do not flow. If, therefore, art teachers were sometimes to deal with visual and plastic representations of other physical types, it might do something to erode racial prejudice. Once a person ceases to say, 'I can't tell one Japanese from another' or, 'All Negroes look alike to me', and instead begins to appreciate the beauty of an almond eye and the delicate sleekness of an ebony skin, he is on the way to overcoming any repugnance to 'yellows' and 'blacks' which may have soaked into him from the atmosphere around. Moreover, a good deal of the apprehension which many children feel about those of different pigmentation stems from a feeling of inadequacy in actual or imagined social intercourse with them, a feeling of inability to recognize the socially significant emotions—of anger and affection and sternness and sympathy—in faces of different colours and conformations. When he has learned to look closely at the faces and gestures of peoples of various ethnic types, and has begun to achieve some degree of confidence in interpreting them, he will no longer accept so readily the stereotypes of the sinister Oriental and the childlike Negro.

Even more valuable in this respect is personal contact under conditions which imply ethnic equality. How effective this may be has been shown[1] in an English school where two Nigerian teachers joined the staff and quite transformed the children's attitude to Negroes. These pupils, as is common in England, had no strong colour prejudice, but many of them found the idea of 'a black man' somewhat disturbing and in a few cases even frightening. However, after being taught by Negro teachers for a while, seeing them accepted by their white colleagues as equal in status and responsibility, getting to understand them and learning at first hand how to interpret their human reactions, almost all the children lost their uneasiness and instead developed a whole-hearted acceptance and liking. This toleration of attitude, moreover, extended from the two teachers to Negroes in general—a result similar to that achieved in other schools where Indian, Chinese and Malayan teachers have taught.

Examples abound to make it clear to children that there is nothing in the nature of things to necessitate racial prejudice. In Brazil, for example, although the early Portuguese introduced large numbers of African slaves as did the British farther north, and although in addition they enslaved the

1. In *The Teacher was Black,* by H. E. O. James and Cora Tenen (Heinemann, London, 1953).

native Amerindians, today the colour-bar is not rigid. True, there is a tendency for more 'Whites' to be in the upper social classes and more 'Blacks' and 'Browns' in the lower; but people of all hues go to school together, travel in the same buses, and when they grow up intermarry with comparatively little chromatic consciousness. There are interesting historical reasons for this state of affairs: the early Portuguese settlers took few women with them and so from the start cohabited with women of other ethnic groups, the Roman Catholic Church to which the Portuguese belonged exerted great pressure to convert irregular sexual unions into regular marriages, the Portuguese had memories of their Moorish overlords of earlier days and so were unable to delude themselves that a darker skin necessarily implied inferior culture or ability, and the slaves of Brazil were freed gradually by many individual acts of manumission—and by decree—rather than by a civil war with its festering sores of memory.

Similarly, in Hawaii, 'Jim Crow' segregation is unknown, and wave upon wave of immigrants from Polynesia, China and Japan, Portugal and Spain, Puerto Rico and the Philippines have been absorbed into a polyethnic society. From time to time there has been prejudice against this or that newcoming group, but always it has weakened and the newcomers have eventually been accepted. In New Zealand, too, despite earlier violent warfare between 'white' and 'black', all today are equal before the law and are granted the same social civilities. And, most instructive, there is the contrast between the behaviour of the Dutch in South Africa and that of their fellow-countrymen in the East Indies. Facts such as these, introduced into geography lessons, will show the pupils that racial prejudice and discrimination are not natural, but man-made phenomena; and what man has made he can unmake.

13. The School and Society

It is a commonplace that what the school can do depends upon the society of which it is a part, and this is especially true in the matter of intergroup relations. Let the teacher say what he will about ethnic equality, his words will be negated by his pupils' everyday experiences in a community which exercises racial or pseudo-racial discrimination. If 'Whites' go to one school and 'Blacks' to another, if children of different hues are segregated in trains or buses, if Gentile teachers will not serve under a Jewish head, the task of the teacher who wishes to eradicate intergroup prejudice is a difficult one. If the clever Negro is not admitted to the local university when he leaves school, if the Jewish child who wishes to become a doctor or lawyer is excluded from professional teaching under a *numerus clausus,* then the best lessons on ethnic origins will tend to look somewhat foolish. If, as in South Africa and many states of the U.S.A., marriage between 'black' and 'white' is illegal, and to many people virtually unthinkable, then reference to the brilliance of individual Negroes will not be specially effective.

This, however, is not a counsel of despair; it is merely an incentive to greater effort. Naturally, the teacher has to take account of local prejudices and in some cases of local laws, but he need not supinely repress his own better feelings and his own response to reason. He can often make clear his own disapproval of discriminatory laws and customs, and that will mean a lot to his pupils who respect him. Even in districts with segregated school systems, it may be possible to arrange inter-school visits and joint out-of-school activities, to discuss with the class the historical reasons for and the ethics of segregation, and to encourage the parents of the pupils from the different schools to establish friendly personal relations. Just how forthrightly he will speak and act each individual teacher must decide for himself, and in some cases he may suffer for his plain speaking; but no great cause was ever won without some sacrifice. And, if the teacher is as tactful as he is honest, he can usually avoid any major trouble.

What must most concern the teacher is not the risk of some slight social inconvenience to himself, but rather that of some perhaps considerable emotional damage to his pupils. When he seeks to liberate a child from racial prejudice, he must take care not to alienate the child from his probably prejudiced parents; when he sets out to strengthen the self-esteem of a child suffering discrimination, he must take care not to hang about his neck the millstone of martyrdom. While he is protesting against the prejudices of his pupils' parents, he must ensure that he is not imposing a type of school discipline which fosters those frustrations on which intolerance feeds. While he is protecting children from acts of racial discrimination and manifestations of racial prejudice, he needs to avoid that over-protection which will leave the children quite defenceless once they are outside the school. He will encourage children of all ethnic origins to work and play amicably together, but will not force the issue to a point where resentments are aroused and intolerance merely driven sullenly underground. And, if the teacher is to have a fair chance to do all this, society must provide the money for suitable school buildings and for classes small enough to permit the abandonment of authoritarian disciplinary methods.

The teacher of children belonging to minority groups, such as Negro children in New York or Jewish children in London or Mexican ones in Los Angeles, has a peculiarly delicate task. He must do what he can to provide constructive outlets for his pupils' emotional drives, so that they do not become blocked by the barriers of racial prejudices, and fester unseen below. He must honestly present to his pupils the peculiarities of their position so as to prepare them for their life in the community, but in such a way as to arouse a determination to right wrongs rather than a tendency to nourish a sour sense of grievance. He must show sympathy with children in their righteous resentment at discrimination, but the sympathy must not encourage them to blame the social order for their own personal shortcomings. In short, he must strengthen and not violate the integrity of his pupils' personalities.

Care must be taken, too, not to evoke uncertainty and fear where they do not already exist. To explain to a child, gently and calmly and dispassionately, how it has happened that an unpleasant incident has occurred, and to smooth away the pain with love and affection, is one thing; to worry a child prematurely about all sorts of hypothetical incidents which may perhaps never happen and so make unnecessary cracks in his confidence, is quite another. The Jewish child in Berlin or Paris or London may be encouraged to take pride in his people's heritage, but not at the cost of accentuating any feeling that he is fundamentally different from the 'Goy'. The Negro child in Atlanta or Knoxville or New York may be told about the achievements of Negroes in Nigeria, but not in such a way as to imply that his proper place is anywhere but the U.S.A. If teachers were habitually to speak not of 'German Jews' and 'American Negroes', but rather of 'Jewish Germans' and 'Negro Americans', things would be put in better perspective. If children of any minority group become ashamed of their origin, try to hide it, and begin to develop a sort of split personality, it will be harmful not only to them but to their whole school class. It is therefore a task of great importance for the teacher to do what he can to liberate his wards from inferiority feelings of this sort and from the distorting effects of the defence mechanisms which minority children so often develop.

In all this, however, co-operation with the community at large is essential; and, in particular, co-operation with the pupils' parents, both in parent-teacher associations and as individuals. The number of people who are proud of their prejudices is comparatively small: the majority are so ashamed of them that they hide them even from themselves, and few would consciously wish their children to be prejudiced. If the teachers in a school will take the trouble to talk things over with such parents, not attacking them and so arousing resistance, but calmly proffering partnership in overcoming a common enemy, many will respond. Gently, tactfully, little by little, parents can be persuaded to improve their own practices and those of the community as a whole. Mrs. A may agree to invite a child of different colour to come home for tea with her own children, Mr. B may agree to refrain from telling 'funny' stories about 'yids' and 'wops' and 'chinks', the C family who are 'white' and the D family who are 'black' may agree to go out swimming together. And, in all such things, the teachers themselves may set the example.

The actual school lessons, too, may reach out into the wider community. A predominantly Gentile class may pay a visit to a synagogue and learn something of the rich cultural heritage of the Jews; a predominantly Jewish class may visit a Christian church. When the children of a minority religion are absent for a religious holiday, its significance may be explained to their classmates; contrariwise, the minority group pupils may be instructed in the elements of the beliefs of the majority. With older pupils, it may even be possible to make a study of comparative religion. And, in this way, a child may learn that those of other faiths are not just stubbornly refusing to accept his own religion, but that they have firmly held religious convictions of their own. In other schools, a field study may be made of an ethnically mixed neighbourhood where peoples of different colours and different faiths live in harmony together, and out of such a project there may develop all sorts of interesting class discussions and individual reorientations. And, in all the many ways which will occur to the teacher, an effort may be made to ensure that what the children learn about race at school is seen to be relevant to the community at large.

Local community study, intelligently conceived and carefully executed, can be of the utmost value. Without intelligence and care on the part of the teacher, however, they may do as much harm as good. Thus, for example, a class visit to a Negro slum might tend to reinforce rather than dissipate the prejudices of children too immature to distinguish the effects of poverty from those of pigmentation, while a casual walk round a predominantly Chinese neighbourhood might accentuate awareness of superficial cultural characteristics instead of emphasizing the kinship of all mankind. Yet, with proper preparation, these same studies can be illuminating and liberating experiences for the pupils.[1] Prejudices can be brought out into the open, problems posed for intensive investigation, material collected relevant to questions which have arisen in the classroom before the visits, observations discussed and confusions clarified in discussion after the visits, personal contacts made and maintained by groups of children and by individuals, and social skills developed in dealing with those of different ethnic origins and cultural backgrounds.

Yet—such, regrettably, is the stubbornness of human error—it is not unknown for children to agree in classroom discussions that racial discrimination is wrong and racial prejudice irrational, and even to learn in community study a good deal about the factors influencing race relations, and none the less to continue in their daily lives to exercise discrimination and display prejudice in all sorts of little ways. There is a Chinese proverb which may be approximately rendered, 'If I hear, I forget; if I see, I remember; if I do, I know'; and it is in *action* against racial wrongs that children really learn racial rightness. Once a child has actually committed himself by asserting his friendship for a schoolmate of different colour, once he has argued with his playmates that a child hitherto racially rejected should be admitted to their games, he has become emotionally involved in the struggle for racial equality and has innerly identified himself with those who insist on racial tolerance. Thus, if the teacher can, without ever pressing any individual to the point of resentment, encourage his pupils not merely to talk about but actively to take part in a programme of non-discrimination, he may achieve something which no amount of mere moral exhortation can bring about. A class committee could be appointed to draft a letter to the publisher of a textbook which misrepresents a particular ethnic group or to congratulate the manager of a cinema which shows a film meritorious in its ethnic outlook; a group of children about to leave school may

1. See *Our East London: How We Came Here* and *Our East London: the Growth of its Religions* (Council of Citizens of East London, London, 1949).

be encouraged to help in finding a job for a classmate whose colour or religion places obstacles in his way; the half dozen or so pupils who are the accepted leaders of the class may be persuaded to see to it that none of their classmates are rejected from recreative activities on racial or pseudo-racial grounds. Before many years have passed, the pupils of the secondary school will be adult citizens of the community, and while at school they should learn ethnic equality not merely by precept but in practice.

In this connexion, it is essential to remember that children, like their elders, are commonly reluctant to act alone. The individual with the courage to flout the herd is a priceless asset to a community, for without such individuals a society ossifies. It is, however, unrealistic to expect most pupils to adopt a line of action distasteful to their closest friends; in the main, a child's attitudes and acts are those accepted by his playmates and classmates, his 'peer-group'. Recognizing this, the teacher who wishes to alter behaviour will normally seek to influence the whole group rather than an individual in isolation. In connexion with ordinary school discipline, this is taken for granted; all children, not just a few, are taught to do this and not to do that; and any teacher would recognize the futility of expecting one child to adopt a standard of behaviour markedly higher than that demanded of his fellow-pupils. Precisely the same considerations apply to race relations: in most cases it is simply not realistic to try to prod an individual ahead of his peer-group—indeed, in many cases it would not even be desirable. The attitudes and habitual behaviour of the whole group must be improved if any but the most independent children are to be appreciably affected. That is why group discussions and group projects, even if at times they appear to be very time-consuming, are in the long run most influential in producing changes.

Yet the child is not constrained absolutely by his peer-group; the behaviour of respected adults can set a most effective example. If teachers seem to contract out of the social situation, pupils can scarcely be blamed for doing likewise. If teachers demonstrate by their actions their concern for social righteousness, pupils will be encouraged to do the same.

Finally, therefore, the teacher should have the temerity to exercise his citizen rights. All too often, in many lands, teachers tend to be somewhat retiring, spending their evenings and week-ends with a few choice friends, themselves not infrequently teachers too. Only rarely do they join in the casual conversations of the local café or public house, take part in politics and local government, engage in friendly argument with miners and shopkeepers and engineers. But those who remain within ivory towers can do little to influence the affairs of the great world outside, and the teacher who wishes to help his pupils to a life full and rich and free must be prepared to share in the shaping of the society in which they will live it.

14. Source Material for the Teacher

International

United Nations, New York, U.S.A.; and local representatives and offices in other countries.

Unesco, 19 avenue Kléber, Paris-16e, France; and local representatives and offices in other countries.

World Brotherhood, Centre International, Geneva, Switzerland.

World Jewish Congress, 55 New Cavendish Street, London, W.1.

Great Britain

Africa Bureau, 65 Denison House, Vauxhall Bridge Road, London, S.W.1.

Anti-Slavery Society, Denison House, Vauxhall Bridge Road, London, S.W.1.

Council of Citizens of East London, Toynbee Hall, Commercial Street, London, E.1.

Council of Christians and Jews, 162a Strand, London, W.C.2.

Council for Education in World Citizenship, 25 Charles Street, London, W.1.

East and West Friendship Council, 101 Gower Street, London, W.C.1.
Fellowship of Reconciliation, 29 Great James Street, London, W.C.1.
India League, 47 Strand, London, W.C.2.
Kenya Committee, 86 Rochester Row, London, S.W.1.
League of Coloured Peoples, 3 Robert Street, London, N.W.1.
Racial Relations Group, 20 Grosvenor Court, Acton, London, W.3.
Racial Unity, 32 Denison House, Vauxhall Bridge Road, London, S.W.1.
Royal Anthropological Society, 21 Bedford Square, London, W.C.1.
Royal Institute of International Affairs, Chatham House, London, S.W.1.
Society of Friends (Quakers), Friends House, Euston Road, London, N.W.1.
United Central Africa Association, 25 Lowndes Street, London, S.W.1.

United States of America

American Council on Education, Washington 6, D.C.
Anti-Defamation League of B'nai B'rith, 212 Fifth Avenue, New York 10, N.Y., and 11 Pryor Street S.W., Atlanta, Ga.
Bureau for Intercultural Education, 157 West 13th Street, New York 11, N.Y.
Community Relations Service, American Jewish Committee, 386 Fourth Avenue, New York 16, N.Y.
Congress of Racial Equality, 513 West 166th Street, New York 32, N.Y.
National Association for the Advancement of the Colored Peoples, 20 West 40th Street, New York 18, N.Y.
National Association of Intergroup Relations Officials, 565 North Erie Street, Toledo 2, Ohio.
National Conference of Christians and Jews, 381 Fourth Avenue, New York 16, N.Y
National Urban League, 1133 Broadway, New York 10, N.Y.
Public Affairs Committee, 22 East 38th Street, New York 16, N.Y.
Science Research Associates, 57 West Grand Avenue, Chicago 10, Ill.
Social Science Research Council, 230 Park Avenue, New York 17, N.Y.
Southern Regional Council, 63 Auburn Avenue N.E., Atlanta 3, Ga.

Bibliography

Literature on racial relations is very extensive. This bibliography only contains books of a general character which have appeared in fairly recent years and which are easily available in libraries and bookstores.

PUBLICATIONS OF THE UNITED NATIONS AND UNESCO

The main types and causes of discrimination (memorandum submitted by the Secretary General). United Nations Commission on Human Rights, Lake Success, New York, 1949.

The Universal Declaration of Human Rights: a guide for teachers, 1953—lists many books, booklets, filmstrips, etc., which will be of value to the teacher.

History textbooks and international understanding, by J. A. Lauwerys, 1953.

A handbook of suggestions on the teaching of geography (Towards world understanding—X*),* 1951.

In the classroom with children under thirteen years of age (Towards world understanding—V*),* 1949.

The race question in modern science—a series of simple but authoritative booklets, as follows:

Race and culture, by Michel Leiris, 1951.
Race and psychology, by Otto Klineberg, 1951.
Race and biology, by L. C. Dunn, 1951.
Racial myths, by Juan Comas, 1951.
The roots of prejudice, by Arnold M. Rose, 1951.
Race and history, by Claude Lévi-Strauss, 1952.
Race and society, by Kenneth L. Little, 1952.
The significance of racial differences, by G. M. Morant, 1952.
The race concept. Results of an inquiry, 1952.
Race mixture, by Harry L. Shapiro, 1953.

The race question and modern thought—a similar series, as follows:

The Catholic Church and the race question, by Father Yves M.-J. Congar, O.P., 1953.
Jewish thought as a factor in civilization, by Leon Roth, 1954.
The ecumenical movement and the race problem, by W. A. Visser't Hooft, 1954.

Race and society—a similar series, as follows:

Race and class in rural Brazil, by Charles Wagley, 1952.
Les élites de couleur dans une ville brésilienne, by Thales de Azevedo, 1953.

Racial equality and the law, by Morroe Berger, 1954.
Contacts de civilisations en Martinique et en Guadeloupe, by Michel Leiris.

OTHER PUBLICATIONS

Race and Science

Mankind so far, by William W. Howells. New York, Doubleday; London, Sigma; 1947.
The new you and heredity, by Amram Scheinfeld. Philadelphia, Lippincott; London, Chatto and Windus; 1950.
Heredity and politics, by J. B. S. Haldane. London, Allen and Unwin, 1938.
We Europeans, by J. S. Huxley, A. C. Haddon and A. M. Carr-Saunders. London, Penguin, 1939.
Man's most dangerous myth: the fallacy of race, by M. F. Ashley Montagu. New York, Columbia University Press, 1952, 3rd ed.
Race: a study in modern superstition, by Jacques Barzun. New York, Harcourt Brace, 1937.

Human Relations Generally

Human rights, a symposium, edited by Unesco. London and New York, Allan and Wingate, 1949.
Our east London: how we came here and *Our east London: the growth of its religions.* Council of Citizens of East London, 1949.
Intergroup education in public schools, by Hilda Taba, Elizabeth Hall Brady and John T. Robinson. Washington, American Council on Education, 1952.
This is the general report on a comprehensive project which is described in more detail in the following books, all from the same publisher:
Reading ladders for human relations.
Literature for human understanding.
Sociometry in group relations.
Elementary curriculum in intergroup relations.
Curriculum in intergroup relations: secondary.
With focus on human relations.
The same publisher is also issuing a series of *Studies in intergroup relations,* also mainly by Hilda Taba.
A decade of groupwork, ed. C. E. Hendry. New York, Association Press, 1948.
Living without hate, by Alfred Marrow, New York, Harper, 1951.

The Negro People

The Negro's struggle for survival, by S. J. Holmes. San Francisco, University of California Press, 1937.
Documents illustrative of the history of the slave trade to America, by Elizabeth Dunnan. Washington, D.C., Carnegie Institute, 1930.
The myth of the Negro past, by Melville J. Herskovits, New York, Harper, 1941.
The Negro in American life and thought: the nadir 1877-1901, by Rayford W. Logan. New York, Dial Press, 1954.
Progress in Negro status and race relations, 1911-1946, by Anson Phelps Stokes. New York, Phelps-Stokes Fund, 1948.
An American dilemma: the Negro problem and modern democracy, by Gunnar Myrdal. New York, Harper, 1944.
The Protestant Church and the Negro, by Frank Loescher. New York, Association Press, 1948.
Negroes in Britain: a study of racial relations in English society, by K. L. Little. London, Kegan Paul, 1948.
Colour prejudice, by Alan Burns. London, Allen and Unwin, 1948.
Colour prejudice in Britain, by Anthony H. Richmond. London, Routledge, 1954.
The teacher was black, by H. E. O. James and Cora Tenen. London, Heinemann, 1953.

The Jewish People

Must men hate?, by Sigmund Livingston. Cleveland, Crane Press, 1944.
Antisemitism through the ages, by H. Coudenhove-Kalergi. London, Hutchinson, 1935.
Overcoming anti-Semitism, by Solomon A. Fineberg. New York, Harper, 1943.
Judaism in the first century of the Christian era, by J. F. Moore. Cambridge, Cambridge University Press, 1930.
Jewish holidays and festivals, by Ben M. Edidin. New York, Hebrew Publishing Co., 1940.
The Jewish people—past and present. 3 vols. New York, Jewish Encyclopaedia Handbooks, 1946-52.
A short history of the Jewish people, by Cecil Roth. Oxford, East and West Library, 1953 ed.
The Jews: their history, culture and religion, ed. Louis Finkelstein. 2 vols. New York, Harper, 1949.

Minorities and Race Relations Generally

The Mexican immigrant: his life story, by Manuel Gamio. Chicago, University of Chicago Press, 1930.
They came from Japan, by Bradford Smith. Philadelphia, Lippincott, 1948.

Racial and cultural minorities, by G. E. Simpson and J. M. Yinger. New York, Harper, 1953.

American minority peoples, by Donald R. Young. New York, Harper, 1932.

Interracial marriage in Hawaii, by Romanzo Adams. New York, Macmillan, 1937.

Caste and race in India, by G. S. Ghurye. London, Kegan Paul, 1932.

Race attitudes in South Africa, by I. D. MacCrone. London, Oxford University Press, 1937.

The trouble-makers, by Arnold Foster and Benjamin Epstein. New York, Doubleday, 1952.

Action for unity, by Goodwin Watson. New York, Harper, 1947.

Colour conflict, by A. Broomfield. London, Edinburgh House, 1943.

Race relations in a democracy, by Ira C. Brown. New York, Harper, 1949.

Handbook on racial relations, ed. Ellen Hellman. London, Oxford University Press, 1949.

Half-caste, by Cedric Dover. London, Secker and Warburg, 1937.

Miscellaneous

Straight and crooked thinking, by R. H. Thoules. London, Hodder, 1936.

A peoples' history of England, by A. L. Morton. London, Gollancz, 1938.

Who shall be educated?, by W. Lloyd Warner, Robert J. Havighurst and Martin B. Loeb, New York, Harper; London, Kegan Paul; 1944.

Patterns of culture, by Ruth Benedict. Boston, Mifflin, 1934; London, Routledge, 1935.

Sex and temperament in three primitive societies, by Margaret Mead. New York, Morrow, 1935.

The authoritarian personality, by T. W. Adorno *et al.* New York, Harper, 1950.

Dynamics of prejudice, by Bruno Bettelhein and Morris Janowitz. New York, Harper, 1952.

The nature of prejudice, by Gordon W. Allport. Cambridge (Mass.), Addison-Wesley, 1954.

(1) The fact — which is of
is the ... [illegible]
Sexuality

(2) Local ... [illegible]
... [illegible]
by ... [illegible]

(3) Impact Race relations
Otherwise
race etc
and forms

Basis: (1) ... [illegible]
(2) ... is one
(3) others

At the base of all prejudice is
an Ethnic ... [illegible] by
the ... [illegible]